# Laughter through Tears

**SARA F. YOSELOFF MEMORIAL PUBLICATIONS**
In Judaism and Jewish Affairs

This volume is one in a series established in memory
of Sara F. Yoseloff,
who devoted her life to the making of books.

# Laughter through Tears

*The Yiddish Cinema*

Judith N. Goldberg

Rutherford • Madison • Teaneck
Fairleigh Dickinson University Press
London and Toronto: Associated University Presses

© 1983 by Associated University Presses, Inc.

Associated University Presses, Inc.
4 Cornwall Drive
East Brunswick, N.J. 08816

Associated University Presses Ltd
27 Chancery Lane
London WC2A 1NS, England

Associated University Presses
Toronto M5E 1A7, Canada

**Library of Congress Cataloging in Publication Data**

Goldberg, Judith N., 1950–
 Laughter through tears.

 Bibliography: p.
 Filmography: p.
 Includes index.
 1. Moving-pictures, Yiddish—History.  I. Title.
PN1995.9.Y54G6       791.43′09       80-70900
ISBN 0-8386-3074-X                    AACR2

*Printed in the United States of America*

*To Hannah and Irving Goldberg*

# Contents

|  |  | Page |
|---|---|---|
| Illustrations | | 9 |
| Preface | | 11 |
| Acknowledgments | | 13 |
| 1 | Introduction | 17 |
| 2 | 1910 to World War I | 27 |
| 3 | World War I to the Coming of Sound | 43 |
| 4 | 1929–1934: The Yiddish Talkie | 57 |
| 5 | The Yiddish Cinema in America | 74 |
| 6 | The Yiddish Cinema in Poland | 104 |
| 7 | Aftermath | 116 |
| Notes | | 121 |
| Bibliography | | 127 |
| Filmography | | 133 |
| Index | | 161 |

# Illustrations

| | |
|---|---:|
| *Laughter through Tears* | 49 |
| *East Side Sadie* | 63 |
| *Zein Weibs Lubonvnik* | 65 |
| *The Eternal Jew* | 69 |
| *Chalutzim* | 69 |
| *Tevya* (poster) | 76 |
| *The Jewish Melody* | 80 |
| *Motel the Operator* | 82 |
| *Green Fields* | 85 |
| *The Singing Blacksmith* | 90 |
| *Americaner Shadchen* | 92 |
| *Where Is My Child?* | 96 |
| *Tevya* | 98 |
| *Without a Home* | 111 |
| *Jolly Paupers* | 111 |
| *The Dybbuk* | 113 |
| *Mazel Tov Yidden* | 119 |

# Preface

Yiddish films have once again become popular because of the recent acceptance and rediscovery of Yiddish culture and the growing interest in all types of film. The ethnic Yiddish heritage is no longer the embarrassment it was to the recently assimilated Jews of the past few decades. Yiddish is once more a real language with its own artistic body of work. Those who once would have been horrified by the outright sentimentality, the conservative ethics, and the technical crudeness of Yiddish films now attend them for their historical value as an excellent picture of immigrant Jewish life, the superb acting, and the simple fact that most of these films are very good entertainment. There is now an annual Yiddish film festival in New York City. The first Yiddish film festival in Los Angeles was so popular that it was repeated, and these films play to sold-out theaters, synagogues, and museums throughout the United States.

Most of these films come from the Rutenberg and Everett Collection of the National Center for Jewish Film in association with the American Jewish Historical Society and Brandeis University in Waltham, Massachusetts. This small institution is run by three devoted women: Sharon Pucker Rivo, Miriam Krant, and Rhoda Alper.

The R & E Film Library is a more or less self-supporting institution, barely making ends meet through its only source of income—film rentals. But film rentals are only a part of its function, for it is responsible for the collection and preservation of Yiddish films. At this writing, it has managed to find some 50 of an estimated 130 made; but funds have been available to restore only 10 of them. For only a few films, the library has special program notes describing their historical and cultural background.

It costs anywhere from $10,000 to $20,000 to restore one film. This depends on the starting material, which in many cases is only a 16mm print, and many of the prints are in such poor condition that no new titles can be added but only a copy made. The American Film Institute was at first able to fund the library under their film preservation program, but money is no longer available. The AFI is storing the negatives and 35mm nitrate prints for the R & E Library in their vaults in Washington, and as more of the films are found, they go into these vaults.

The Rutenberg and Everett Yiddish Film Library is treating these films with the respect they deserve. But it is a battle against time as it seeks the funds to find and then preserve these films. They are in desperate need of money. Often the R & E Library is so short of funds that it is unable to make prints needed to fulfill the demand for the films.

In order that these films may be seen in their context, I have presented information on the condition of the Jews in their respective countries and have included background information on the film industries. All spellings of names and films are common usage.

# Acknowledgments

This project began as a master's thesis in 1975, and I would like to thank all the people who have helped me. My apologies and thanks to any I have forgotten.

   In particular, I wish to thank Dr. Knudson and the staff of Special Collections at the Doheny Library, University of Southern California; the reference and microfilm staff, Doheny Library; the staff of the Academy of Motion Pictures Arts & Sciences, Margaret Herrick Library; the Library of Congress, the New York Public Library, Harvey and Cheryl at Hebrew Union College, Avraham Schenker and the Rad Archives at the University of Jerusalem, Esther Eng at the Museum of the City of New York, the Yiddish Scientific Institute, Shalom Altman, Gratz College; Stuart Fox, Paul Spehr, Anthony Slide, Sam Gill, the UCLA Theatre Arts Library, Richard Koszarski, Audrey Kupferberg at the American Film Institute, Priscilla Rockwell; Robert van Laer, Dr. Louis Cohen, Edward Kaufman, Abraham Zygielbaum, Irwin Blacker, Arthur Knight, Ellen Kaufman; and especially Joseph Green, David Opatoshu, Harold Seiden, Leo Fuchs, Herschel Bernardi, and Sharon Pucker Rivo, and Miriam Krant and Rhoda Alpher at the Rutenberg and Everett Yiddish Film Library, without whom this would not have been possible.

# Laughter through Tears

# 1 Introduction

The last new Yiddish film was released in 1961. Between the years 1910 and 1941, approximately 130 feature films and 30 short films were made in the Yiddish language. That such a small body of work, produced in four countries and scattered over a period of thirty years, should have been ignored is easily understood. Records are poor and memories are faulty. A single Hollywood movie company often made more than this number of films in a few years. *Film Daily Yearbook, 1942* lists over 18,000 films produced worldwide from 1915 to 1941, yet less than half of these Yiddish films appear on the list. Yiddish films survived only in the memories of those who saw them.

A second- or third-generation Jewish child, growing up in or near a large metropolitan area in the 1950s and 1960s, probably would hear of some movies in that language which parents often used. Perhaps the local sisterhood presented such a film as a fund-raising event or the relatives trooped to some out-of-the-way movie theater for a similar reason. Strange names—Boris Thomashevsky, Maurice Schwartz, Celia Adler, Yetta Zwerling, Helen Beverly, Isidor Cashier—might be dropped over the dinner table. Perhaps Grandma would then sigh and say, "Ah, just like the old days on Second Avenue, before the war, remember?" Heads would nod in recognition.

Second Avenue, Hastings Street, and Boris Thomashevsky are hardly names recalling the great early days of film. Yet from such people and places a modest film industry once arose. Its roots were not the Samuel Goldwyns, Carl Laemmles, Adolph Zukors, or even D. W. Griffiths, but the once lively and innovative Yiddish theater movement of the United States and Eastern Europe. It grew from the people who lived in and left the *shtetls* of Eastern Europe and tried to keep their culture, language, and memories of home alive.

The Yiddish theater was the major form of popular entertainment available to the Eastern European Jews. Its history is brief. Yiddish theater began in Jassy, Rumania, in 1876 and very quickly developed into a mishmash of historical pageantry, family melodramas, musical comedies, and topical references all tossed together on the stage like chop suey.

When the Jewish mass immigration from Eastern Europe began during the 1880s, many of the actors and playwrights were included in the movement. Ranging from South America to South Africa and of course the United States, Yiddish theater flourished wherever the Eastern European Jews settled. The larger European cities had had resident companies (such as the Vilna Troupe and the Warsaw Art Theater); smaller cities were also visited by traveling troupes and often had serious amateur companies of their own. This now continued in the United States. After the first performance of Yiddish theater in New York in 1882, every major city soon had at least one professional Yiddish theater group, and at one time, New York City had twenty-three.

Yiddish theater, though dependent on *shund* ("trash") for its bread and butter, went through two periods of serious works and experimentation—in the 1890s and in 1918—before its ultimate decline in the 1930s.

From this theatrical background, the Yiddish fim emerged. There were the experimental films from the Soviet Union; the careful, serious productions of the Polish art theaters; the sentimental American musical comedies, the pious cantorials, historical melodramas of the teens, the topical intelligent modern works, and the melodramas of immigrant life. They were made in the United States, Poland, Austria, and the Soviet Union.

Theater and then cinema embraced the entire gamut of Yiddish culture. The two million Jews who left Eastern Europe for the United States from 1881 to 1924 and those who remained had a distinct culture, the culture of *Yiddishkeit*. Despite the absence of a common homeland or territory, the contemporary Jewish community was held together by historical, cultural, and religious ties.

Created primarily for an audience whose native language was Yiddish, the genre of Yiddish films also included a number of silent films and several films in Hebrew and English, which were produced under the same circumstances as those in Yiddish, and which catered for identical audiences. All were derived from, based on, and acted by the Yiddish theater.

During the early part of the twentieth century film was a novelty, and its makers were discovering that there were many different types of audiences for their work. One of these was the Yiddish-speaking Jewish population of the world. When conditions were right—economically, socially, historically, and culturally—particular film industries were able to produce for minority audience, to make films that would be of only minor interest to the larger national population. As each nation developed its own film industry, there would be periods of flowering. A record number of films would be made with ample time and money available for experimentation. This still happens today; witness the French New Wave, Italian Neo-Realism, the German New Wave, and the Australian cinema. Whenever this happened in a country with a large Yiddish-speaking population and well-developed Yiddish culture, Yiddish films were made. The history of this Yiddish film production falls into three distinct periods.

During the early years of film production, when movies were just becoming an art, a number of Jewish-oriented films were made. This happened in Russia in 1910, before the Revolution and just as the Russians were setting up their industry. Similarly in Poland, between 1911 and 1914, when filmmakers were feeding the voracious appetite of their country's audience, Yiddish stage productions began to be filmed. In the United States, from 1913 to 1915, when the Motion Picture Patents Company was losing its stranglehold on the American film industry, the independents were flourishing, and feature films were just starting to become the norm. However, World War I, which hastened the development of film technology, also brought an end to these films. Imports and exports were curtailed, materials became scarce, and each country drastically cut back production.

After the war and the literal rebuilding of the motion picture industry, once again film production flourished. The most notable revival occurred in the Soviet Union with the newly reorganized and revitalized post-Revolution experimentation of the 1920s. Moviemaking flourished in Austria, briefly, when Austrian filmmakers had their day in the early twenties, and also in Poland in the latter part of the decade. In all these cases, Yiddish literature was adapted to the screen, or Yiddish theatrical actors starred in films plotted around Jewish characters. And in all these countries, anti-Semitism was prevalent. The remainder of the populace had no interest in films about Jews and Jewish life.

In the United States, while European countries made artistic, innovative Yiddish silent films, American filmmakers ignored the Jews. The year 1927 was the peak of Yiddish film production in Poland and the Soviet Union and the year sound came to the American film industry. Thus, while European producers were making Jewish silent films with the skill of three decades, in the United States the film industry was struggling with new technology. Conversely, sound came much later to Europe, and while European technicians of the thirties were grappling with microphones, the American filmmakers were already producing polished sound films.

With the mastery of sound came the luxury of making smaller films for smaller audiences. American audiences were accustomed to seeing two features. Thus the "B" film, the bottom half of the double bill, arose, and with it an entire industry to make these films. Independent producers became proficient in making quick, cheap low-budget films that had a guaranteed audience. The audience for Yiddish films, though, was never very large, even with the addition of an international audience. Thus the Yiddish film industry, small, dominated by one entrepreneur, technically amateurish, and hindered by the lack of a distribution network, flourished throughout the 1930s. It was never to flower in the Soviet Union, for the government's benevolent attitude toward artistic experimentation, and Jewish culture in particular, became more and more repressive as the decade progressed. It took an American, seeing the relative success of American producers and fueled by a desire for profit and "real" Jewish movies, to make films in Poland and create a short-lived Polish Yiddish film industry.

This all ended with World War II. Six million Jews died, and in the crassest economic terms, there was no audience. World War II itself cut back on American independent productions, and in Europe the Nazi invasion eliminated the Polish film industry. Not that the producers didn't try one more time in 1950, both in the United States and within the newly formed Film Polski, but it was too late.

The death of the Yiddish film is tied to the temporary demise of *Yiddishkeit,* whether by forceful eradication or voluntary assimilation. It took a thousand years to shape this culture and language. The Soviet Union strangled it with impossible laws and diluted and shaped it to fit another ideology. Hitler stopped it completely in its natural habitat of Eastern Europe by killing its people. The United States took the Eastern European immigrants and assimilated them. Though the American Jews gave up their culture willingly, it was changed nonetheless.

For the immigrants in the years after they moved to America and other countries and for those Jews who remained in Europe, the films fullfilled a need, as with the Yiddish theater, to have their own entertainment. Silent films were universal, but it was the sound film, ignoring Jews, that spawned the true Yiddish film. Joseph Seiden and other independent producers gave these people what they wanted: films in Yiddish about the working-class immigrant striving for a better life. These were the same as the plays one could see on Second Avenue, cheap, trashy melodramas, but they were movies. There were even art films as there were art plays, often the very same plays. For those who still lived in the ethnic ghettos, the films were a very modern and inexpensive way to pass the time. For those Jews who moved out to the suburbs of New York City or across the United States, this was the Yiddish theater they left behind or only dropped by on an occasional tour. For the Jewish immigrants scattered throughout the world, such as the South African and South American Jews, the films filled the gaps between the touring Yiddish theater troupes. They no longer had to wait for the annual tour from the United States or Poland to see their plays. For countries like Poland with thriving (albeit shrinking) Jewish communities, these films were, unlike the Polish products, "theirs"—in their language and made by their people. And with the increasing deterioration of the status of the European Jews in the thirties, they were also a source of comfort.

When the Yiddish theater began, it reflected the mores of the Eastern European Jews and their problems, religious attitudes, and human values. This theater came to America with the immigrants. The immigrants changed as they began to participate in the social, cultural, and economic currents of American life. They strove to "better" their children. The first generation kept their culture. The second generation sought total integration with America and became estranged from the language. The young people eschewed identification with traditional Jewish cultural activities and fled from the ghetto culture and spiritual life. By the 1940s many of the first generation of Yiddish-speaking Americans had died. No new immigrants replaced them. The second generation of American Jews had been assimilated, and though they remained Jewish, they no longer retained the Eastern European Yiddish culture.

Those immigrants and second-generation Jews attending

Yiddish theater in the 1930s were watching the hollow memories of the past. They clung to their traditions, and these traditions were in turn glorified by the theater and films. Since there were no new immigrants, the audience could only watch and wait to die.

The films showed this. They had a very small audience that was easily satisfied. All one had to do was copy what was showing on the stage. Certainly with such a limited audience there was not very much money to spend on the technical aspects of production, and the films might be as bad as a home movie. The films were never better than the movies being made in the mainstream of production; at their best, they were as good. Low budgets were not the only reason for their poor technical quality—basically, no one cared. Joseph Seiden could always find an audience for some tangled tale of lost children and abused parents that featured singing and dancing and a happy ending. A filmed performance of the Warsaw Art Theater, repeating some classic play, filled the theaters the same as did their tours with the "real" thing the immigrants had left behind. The actors rarely took these films seriously, and for most of them it was a matter of quick money, an extra job, to be done when the season was over or in between rehearsals. They were in and out in a few hours.

The war destroyed the Jewish communities in Europe and the fountain of genuine Jewish creativity in Europe. No longer could the old-style Yiddish films satisfy the new demands of the changed taste of the American Jewish community, now the largest and most important in the world. You cannot sell tickets to a nonexistent audience. This is a predicament dating back to the thirties. As David Opatoshu summed it up, "They needed a very young actor who spoke Yiddish fluently and there weren't too many around. Very young ones that is."

During the Jewish settlement of Palestine, Yiddish became a symbol of the very diaspora that the Zionists were trying to escape. The leaders, though fluent in Yiddish themselves and raised in its traditions, encouraged the speaking of Hebrew as a means of breaking with the past. However, they did not ignore the language, and from the beginning they offered awards to its artists. After the war, many of the surviving Eastern European Jews immigrated to Israel, where a great deal of the culture was able to gain a new foothold and continue. There was one major exception—the theater. Considerable interest and benevolence toward "Mama Yiddish" is the rule in present-day Israel. Prizes are awarded for the best creations in poetry and prose. But while Yiddish theatrical performances continue, they have degenerated to the worst *shund* of Second Avenue. As in the United States, the creative, changing Yiddish theater and along with it the films, are dead.

The rebirth of interest in Yiddish culture has come too late to revive the Yiddish theater and cinema. The present interest is a looking back, a rediscovery and reassimilation of a past that was so casually discarded a few decades before. The purpose that the films and theater served, of entertainment to the lonely and homesick immigrants and the European Jewish community, is gone. The films have become records of a different time. Any film that comes out of this rediscovery of Yiddish culture will have to reflect this.

The films are dead and, until very recently, completely forgotten. So, why bother with a study of Yiddish films? Did these films really have any effect on filmmaking and film history? To the latter question, unfortunately, the answer is: probably not very much. The language in which the films were made limited their audience so much that even the handful of really fine films had only a very small circulation. Norman Jewison does claim that he studied the 1937 *Yiddle with His Fiddle* for his production of *Fiddler on the Roof*, but this is an exception.

The label *Yiddish* became a stigma that caused the films to be deliberately forgotten. A number of people who went on to modest careers in the major film industries of their respective countries worked in these films. Edgar G. Ulmer is the best-known of the directors, yet his four Yiddish films have never been included in critical studies of his work. Douglas Shearer, the ubiquitous MGM soundman, worked on one of the early films. Joseph Berne had a brief career in Hollywood. Alexis Granowski directed in Europe. Ossip Dymov wrote screenplays. Max Nosseck directed "B" features. J. Burgi Cotner had a long career as a cinematographer. Leo Fuchs and David Opatoshu are well-respected actors. Jan-Nowina Przybilski and Michael Wasynski have extensive Polish screen credits. Nicholas Brodsky composed for MGM. This is not a very long list; most actors stayed in the Yiddish theater. It has been so many years since anyone has thought about these films that their possible influence has never been acknowledged. How many people currently working on films, or who have worked in the motion picture industry in the past, were first introduced to movies with *My Yiddishe Mama?*

The theatrical basis of these films acts as a historical record of the Yiddish theater, which did have an influence on mainstream theater. Here forever is the performance of the great Boris Thomashevsky, matinee idol of the Yiddish stage; of Maurice Schwartz, pioneer of naturalism; Shlomo Mikhoels, one of the greatest Russian-Jewish actors; the Kaminsky Troupe; Molly Picon performing the type of work that made her famous, the satirical sketches of Dzigan and Schumacher; Moishe Oysher's great baritone; and Isidor Cashier and Abraham Lax, two great character actors. Paul Muni's earliest stage training was with Maurice Schwartz's Jewish Art Theater; captured forever in later films of *Tevya* and *Uncle Moses.*

Even more than the theatrical record, the films' value lies in their record of the past. They have recorded all the hopes, joys and disappointments of the Eastern European Jews as they saw their lives changing. The films are invaluable for a statement of Eastern European Jewish morality, their reliance on the past, and of the difficulty in adjusting to a new life. They also form a record of the diversity of the Yiddish language, from the textbook clarity of the Polish theatrical productions to the relaxed speech of the American films. Some of the films are a glorious celebration of the traditional past, such as *The Dybbuk.* Others, like *Tevya* and *The Light Ahead,* reflect the emptiness of losing that past, the attempt to cling to it, and the fear of change. Still a few show the gradual acceptance of the new, such as *Green Fields* and *Americaner Shadchen*.

And besides this, a review of these films provides us with the story of a people and culture, of what they chose to see on the screen and of how they went about it.

# 2   1910 to World War I

Jews were a popular topic for the early filmmakers.[1] Moreover in the early days of silent movies, companies who wanted to satisfy their audiences had to offer a change of bill several times a week. The output was consequently prolific, and the number of films on all topics was enormous. But to even presume that the few films produced with Yiddish titles, with actors from the Yiddish stage, or by people who later worked in Yiddish sound films had a major impact on audiences places undue importance on this handful of silent films. They were, rather, the roots of a later industry.

Prior to the outbreak of World War I in Europe, Jews were second-class citizens. The inspiration for Jewish films in Russia was the horror of the frequent pogroms. Between the assassination of Alexander II in 1881 and the outbreak of war, approximately one third of all Eastern European Jews emigrated to America. The five million Jews in Russia, out of a total national population in 1897 of 126 million, were restricted to the Pale of Jewish Settlement.[2] The quota for Jewish attendance at the university was only 3 to 7 percent per department. Jews were forbidden to settle outside their present towns and hamlets and were not permitted to carry out any business on Sundays and Christian holidays. The police staged regular raids on Jews found outside the Pale, and these illegal residents were either imprisoned or deported. In some cities, the police doubled the rewards for information on the illicit settlers. The Kiev police were paid from Jewish meat tax revenues.

Anti-Semitism was stepped up as bloody pogroms were carried out in 1881, 1903, and 1905 as the Jews once again served as the scapegoats for the ills of Russian society. For the next ten years, the government encouraged the printing and distribution of 14,237,000 copies of 2,387 anti-Semitic books and pamphlets including the infamous *Prototypes of the Protocols of the Elders of Zion*. In March 1911, following the discovery of the corpse of a thirteen-year-old Russian boy near a Jewish factory in Kiev, the authorities accused Mendel Beilis, a minor Jewish employee in that factory, of ritual murder.

Jewish nationalism of the late nineteenth century generated a cultural renaissance (though it also brought the Bund, a group of Jewish socialists who denied their Jewishness). In poetry there was Chaim Nachman Bialik. In fiction and drama there was Mendele Mocher Seforim (Shalom Jacob Abramovich), father of modern Yiddish letters, Isaac Leib Peretz, and Sholom Aleichem (Solomon Rabinowitz). Russian Yiddish theater, however, was temporarily stifled by an 1883 prohibition of Yiddish public performances, but it managed to survive under the guise of "German" plays until the 1917 abrogation of government prohibitions.

Two French companies, Pathé Frères and Gaumont, dominated pre-Revolution Russian cinema, by first entering distribution (Pathé in 1904), and then becoming the chief Russian producers.[3] Pathé and Gaumont organized business on the outright sale of their projectors and films. By the end of 1904, the cinema business in Moscow had grown from tiny storefront theaters seating 24 and standing 30 to palaces seating 500.

The czar had direct control over the cinema industry. No films of the 1905 uprising ever left the country, and it is assumed that they were destroyed by the government. In April 1906, the government began official censorship of the cinema, along with a tightening of press censorship. One subject was forbidden from the beginning—the French Revolution, together with any showing of the guillotine or of the death of royalty. Gaumont's first widely distributed Russian subject matter films, in 1907, reflected this ban in the blandness of their contents—*The Third State Duma in Session, Review of the Troops by the Royal Family at Tsarskoye Selo, Solemn Procession of Pilgrims at Kiev,* etc.[4] With A. O. Drankov's announcement of the first Russian "Cinematographic Studio" in the autumn of 1907, Russia finally began its own motion picture industry.

By 1910 there were fifteen film studios in Russia including the branch offices of foreign companies. *The Film Index* was able to include Russia in its regular "Motion Pictures in Foreign Countries" column for 28 January 1911.

> The most insignificant towns and villages . . . are well provided with these amusements. . . . In Moscow alone there are about 80 cinematograph theatres and approximately the same number in St. Petersburg. . . . [Orchestras in the foyer] delight the audiences during intermission. . . . French and Italian film companies are controlling the Russian market. . . . The most popular films average 500 to 600 feet; the shortest about 200, and the longest 1,800. . . . The Russians are particularly interested in tragedy and drama. . . . Any event in which a large crowd of people is shown are popular.[5]

Unfortunately, the Russians were unable to watch spectacles about themselves. The infamous League of Russian People became a standard movie villain when a series of pogroms they caused in 1910 was recreated in foreign films but not in Russia. Popularly known as the "Black Hundred," this anti-Semitic group, formed in 1904, functioned with the full support of the Russian government. Among the most famous of these re-creations was *Russia, the Land of Oppression* by Defender films, an American company. Pathé, forbidden to exploit the atrocities of the Russian government on film, was forced to restrict itself instead to making harmless melodramas of Jewish life and then selling them abroad as a true picture of Russian Jewish oppression. *Lai Chyeim* or *Good Luck*, produced in 1910, was the first of these.[6] It was directed by Kai Hansen, one of Pathé's staff directors, with a screenplay by Alexander Arkatov, whose name is later associated with Jewish films.

There is nothing in the plot of *Lai Chyeim* that differentiates it from the standard melodramas of the period. It concerns a young woman, Rachel, who is married off by her father, a rabbi, to wealthy Abraham (Mark, in the British version). She, however, is in love with Abraham's servant, Samuel. After a year of marriage and a daughter, Samuel persuades Rachel to run away with him. She returns to visit Abraham five years later to find him a drunkard and leaves a note telling them that she visited. The *New York Dramatic Mirror* says, "The surroundings and atmosphere of the Jew's life are well maintained and the characters, with the exception of Samuel's, who manifests more energy than expression, are well played."[7]

As the above "Jewish" films prove, there were no real Yiddish films in Russia. There is, of course, the problem that while records of early films are poor, they are especially vague in Russia, both pre- and post-Soviet. Until the Soviets took complete control of the film industry, there were some films with Jewish actors and based on themes taken from Yiddish literature. The most prominent, and well-recorded, is *Lai Chyeim* which was distributed both in Europe and the United States. There are also records of a *King Lear* with Shlomo Mikhoels[8] and of a *Sacrifice of Isaac*.

Alexander Arkatov directed *God of Vengeance (Bog Mesti)* from the play by Sholem Asch. This time Georges Meyer (Joseph Mundviller) wrote the screenplay. In 1913, Arkatov directed *Sorrows of Sarah* with the great Russian star Ivan Mozhukhin, for the Russian company, Khanzhonkov.

From various production companies came some odd phenomena: movies with Yiddish or Hebrew titles and added sound. (This is not as unusual as may appear at first, for experiments with sound films go back to the invention of the phonograph.) Among these oddities are *A Brivele der Mamen (A Little Letter to Mama)*, 1911; *The War and the Jew*, 1914; *Kiddish Hashem*, 1914; and *Beser dem Tot oder aza Shand (Better Death Than Shame)*, 1914. From 20 July 1914 when the czar declared war on Germany, Russian production became heavily war-oriented.

In Poland, the Jews faced similar difficulties to those of their Russian counterparts. Poland, as an independent country existed for only a brief time between the two world wars. When Poland was partitioned among Russia, Austria, and Prussia (in 1795, 1793, and 1772, respectively), the Polish Jews in turn came under the rule of those countries. Each country then exerted its own policy toward the Jews. In the Prussian sector, after 1848, the Jews were granted the right of citizenship, and from then on, the Jews associated themselves with German culture. In Austrian Galicia, they achieved full equality in 1867 and were granted some rights which in later years were augumented. In Russian Poland, Russian legislation against the Jews was in most cases applicable to Poland. And as in Russia, they had to struggle for their very existence. A policy of official state-sponsored anti-Semitism was formulated and Jews were again second-class citizens. It was not until World War I that Jews could even venture on the streets safely.

Despite these restrictions, Yiddish theater flourished. Esther Rachel Kaminska traveled throughout Russia and Poland before and after World War I with the troupe founded by her husband, Avrom Yitskhok Kaminsky, the Kaminsky Troupe. She played both *shund* and art heroines during these years. The Yiddish public and Russian and Polish critics called her the "Jewish Duse." The infant Polish film industry was to find in her plays a wealth of material for the films they so badly wanted to make.

Polish film has one of the oldest traditions in Europe. The first Polish film *Anthony in the Capital,* was directed by Georges Meyer of Pathé. Alexander Hertz also directed for Pathé and sought independence from the Russian producers.

During these formative years, it was difficult to find original screenplays and this is where the Yiddish theater troupes found their place.

Sila ("Strength") Films was one of the earliest companies. It was founded in 1908 by Pawel Goldman, Mojzesz Morak Towbin, and Samuel Ginsberg. Towbin wanted to put the great classics of the Yiddish theater on film and approached the Kaminsky Troupe for permission to film *Der Vilder Fater (Okrutny Ojciec, The Cruel Father)* from the play by Jacob Gordin. Cameras were brought directly to the theater for filming, which is why Ida Kaminska, who appeared in many of them, claims that *Shop on Main Street*, 1966, was her first film. She does not remember. *Der Vilder Fater* starred Zina Goldsztein and Herman Sieracki and was directed by Alexander Marten.

Sila continued productions with *Di Fersztoysene (Wydziedziczeni, The Disinherited)* in 1912, from the play by E. Waksman, directed by Stanislaw Sebel, who had been cameraman on the previous film. The first of what was to be many productions of Gordin's *God, Man and Devil*, became a two-reel film in 1912 with Rudolf Zasawski playing the role of Herschel Dubrowner. *Mirele Efros*, filmed in 1912, starred the entire Kaminsky Troupe. Esther Rachel Kaminska repeated her famous realistic portrayal of Mirele, and Ida Kaminska played the daughter in this four-reel production. Sila declared bankruptcy in 1912.

In 1913, Henryk Finkelstein and Samuel Ginsberg formed Kosmofilm and took over Sila's contracts. They made seven films with the Kaminsky Troupe before World War I closed down production. *Dem Chazons Tochter (Córka Kantora, The Cantor's Daughter)*, produced in 1913, a three-reel adaptation of the Zalmen Libin story, was followed by Jacob Gordin's *Gots Sztrof (Kara Boža, God's Punishment)* and *Der Unbekanter (Nieznajomy, The Stranger)*. *Zajn Wajbs Man (Bigamistka, His Wife's Man)* was also produced in 1913. The final year of production, 1914, saw *Di Sztifmuter (Macocha, The Step-Mother)* and *Di Szchite (Ubój, The Slaughter)*, both from Jacob Gordin plays. All these were directed by Stanislaw Sebel and starred the Kaminsky Troupe. A five-reel *Herecle Mejuches,* from the novel *Przysiega* by Moshe Richter, was also made in 1913, starring the troupe.

The Mintus Company was also filmed. In 1914, Tolstoy's *Masters and Workers* was made in Riga with Mischa Fishzon in the lead. There was also *Yom Hachupa (The Wedding Day)* by Jacob Gordin, *Der Yeshiva Bocher, Dos Pintele Yid,* and *Shma Yisroel.* All were directed by A. Slavinsky. *Hasa Die Yesome (Hasa the Orphan)* was filmed twice, once in 1914 with the Vilna Circle Theater and prior to that by Nahum Lipovsky in Dvinsk.

The Kaminsky Troupe made one last appearance on film, in 1916, in another production of *Zajn Wajbs Man,* the last Polish Yiddish film for a decade.

Polish films were not distributed outside Eastern Europe, except in rare cases. Possibly this was because they were too crude compared to the more sophisticated Danish and English films of the time. A more likely reason is that the companies, Sila and Kosmofilm, were small operations that could not make enough films, on a regular basis, to keep up a steady supply. Only one Polish film was ever advertised in the United States; whether it was shown is a matter for conjecture. *Moving Picture World* of 23 May 1914 had Variety Feature Film Company of New York offering *The Slaughter* by Jacob Gordin "Featuring Mr. S. Adler, Mme. H. Kaminskaia, Supported by an All-Star Cast of Russian-Jewish Players. . . . The Dramatic Sensation of the Jewish Stage in Motion Pictures."[9] If there were any further attempts at selling the Polish films, World War I prevented them.

The refugees fled Europe in three groups: 1881–82, in 1891 after being driven out of Moscow and other Russian cities, and in 1903 after the Kishinev massacre. Between 1901 and 1914, 1,600,000 Jews left Europe, most of them from Russia, Rumania, and Galicia. In all about two million Jews had left Eastern Europe since 1881, and they planned to settle permanently in the United States.

By 1905, the East Side of New York had become a real Jewish community, and there could be no doubt that the most popular form of entertainment was the Yiddish theater. In the early 1900s there were also Jewish vaudeville shows. While the Yiddish press campaigned against what it called vulgar displays, the music halls died a natural death with the birth and increasing popularity of motion pictures. By 1908, as reported in the *Forward,* the immigrant population was flocking to the movie houses. For a nickel, they could see a show, a dance, and hear a song. In 1914, the *Forward* claimed again that the Jews loved the movies.

Films had become a part of American life in the teens. These were the years of the mass creation of stars, the founding of the great motion picture companies, and the gradual construction of the larger motion picture theaters. It was also the period when feature-length films (five reels or more) replaced the one- and two-reel film and the death of the Motion Picture Patents Company, "the Trust."

In 1908, after more than a decade of trying for complete control of the motion picture industry, the Edison Company reached an agreement with the major film manufacturing companies of the day, American Mutoscope and Biograph Company, the Vitagraph Company of America, the Selig Polyscope Company, the Sigmund Lubin Company, Essanay Film Manufacturing Company, the Kalem Company, Pathé Frères and Méliès's Star Film, George Kleine of Chicago, and Thomas Armat. They formed the General Film Company in order to control the distribution of the films they manufactured. The Trust had a rigid schedule of production and a uniform price per foot of film for purchase. Each company was forced to make a certain number of feet of film per week, depending on their size and prior turnout. Feature-length films were strictly forbidden. From the very beginning of the Trust, there were protests by independent theater owners and by a number of independent companies who wanted to compete with the licensed producers.

The Trust took in royalties from every phase of the business. It launched an advertising campaign to ensure that exhibitors booked only Trust films, often convincing them that the independents were not as good. If exhibitors did deal with the independents, they risked having their licenses revoked. Attempts were also made to prevent filming by independent companies, in other words, to put them out of business.

The Trust was successful for about six years. In the end, it lost out to the strong independent companies and the only survivors of the Trust were those that dropped out (like Pathé) or who were eventually taken over by the independents (such as Kalem). In 1915, the federal court declared the Motion Picture Patents Company an illegal conspiracy in restraint of trade.

By 1912, the Trust had begun to weaken and the importation of feature-length films started to attract the middle class to American movie theaters. Construction of the first buildings designed especially for motion pictures began (prior to this storefronts had been used). In Europe, the first such theaters were built in 1911. Nevertheless, movies remained essentially a working-class entertainment until World War I made American movies a giant business. Before the war, Italian, Scandinavian, and French imports had been popular, but with European production curtailed, American film producers filled their own market, and were even ready to export after the war.

Sidney M. Goldin (Golden), later a director of Yiddish talkies, may have been one of the first independent motion picture directors in the United States. Born in Odessa in 1880, he first worked in Chicago with Lincoln J. Carter, the screenwriter, and then with Essanay. In 1912 he was directing gangster films. In February 1913 the Universal Film Company hired him to direct for Victor Feature Film Company and the Imp (Independent Motion Picture Company).[10] The Universal had been formed in 1912 as a loose confederation of several existing companies. Victor Film Company was formed in 1912 by Florence Lawrence, the "Biograph Girl," one of the first screen stars, and by her husband, Harry Salter. It was one of the first companies to feature the work of one star. Its studios were in Fort Lee, New Jersey, as were those of many of the early film companies. Shortly after formation, the Universal took over Victor and by 1913 was hiring other directors and stars.

Goldin's first film for Imp was *The Sorrow of Israel*, released in June 1913. Briefly, the story of this three-reel "special" revolves around a Russian noblewoman and a young Jew, deeply in love with one another. In order to attend university, the young Jew converts. The noblewoman's rejected prince organizes a full-scale "religious persecution" as revenge against the young man. The young Jew is saved by the Nihilists and in gratitude joins them. He marries the noblewoman, lands in jail and is saved again by the Nihilists. The film ends with the happy couple arriving in New York Harbor beneath the Statue of Liberty.[11]

*The Sorrow of Israel* was popular, according to the Universal house organ, the *Universal Weekly* and Mark M. Dintenfass, head of the foreign department and superintendent of the Champion Studios in Coytesville, New Jersey. Plans were made to distribute the film in Europe, aiming for England, Germany, and Austria but not Russia. "On the whole, I rather expect that it will be a greater success than anything yet produced here and sent abroad."[12]

*Nihilist Vengeance*, two reels, followed from Victor. This film too supervised by Mark Dintenfass, but this time the girl was the daughter of a Jewish banker and the lover is a young Christian prince. Oddly, after much intrigue with the Nihilists and the inevitable arrest, the father gives his blessings for a marriage between his daughter and the prince.[13]

The Nihilists portrayed in these films never existed. Originally a philosophy of skepticism when the movement began in the nineteenth century, during the decade 1860 to 1870, they were erroneously associated with the regicide and political terror of the times. By the twentieth century the movement had evolved into a symbol of the struggle against all forms of tyranny. Filmmakers like Sidney Goldin were able to use ignorance to create a popular and romantic cause.

For his third film for the Universal, Goldin dealt "with the intimate life of the Russian Jewish immigrant in America."¹⁴ In *The Heart of a Jewess,* a young Russian Jewish girl, Rebecca, finds work in a garment factory. The foreman falls in love with her but she spurns him for her sweetheart, Jake, who is to come from Russia. Jake duly arrives and Rebecca sends him to medical school with her savings. When he graduates, he drops her for a rich match. On the way to the synagogue for the wedding, the couple run over Rebecca. In the hosital her lover begs her forgiveness but Rebecca tells him to go to his waiting bride, who then spurns him. The foreman returns and marries Rebecca.¹⁵ According to one critic, *The Heart of a Jewess* stars "some of the best Jewish actors obtainable in America."¹⁶

*Moving Picture World* praised *The Heart of a Jewess.*

> It is a pleasure to see Jewish people play Hebrew roles of comedy and sympathy, especially after so many sickening caricatures have affronted vaudeville audiences for years. . . . He [the Hebrew] is presented as he is in the raw material as a beginner in a new environment. . . . In this presentation of exact conformity to truth, there is plainly exhibited both the Hebrew's inability to discern progress in a change of custom and the readiness with which he adapts himself to harsh circumstances.¹⁷

The review goes on to praise the authenticity of the sweatshop and poverty depicted and the quality of the plot and acting.

*Bleeding Hearts or Jewish Freedom under King Casimir of Poland,* three reels, released in October 1913, marked Goldin's final major production for the Universal. Again Goldin worked under Mark Dintenfass. Irene Wallace starred in this semihistorical tale. Universal claimed, "it is perfectly natural to find in Miss Wallace, of mingled Scotch and Irish blood, a young lady who combines all the ideals of Jewish maidenhood on the motion picture stage. . . . One of the things that especially seem to confirm the old Pictish legends that the modern Scotch and Irish are descendents of the Seven Lost

Tribes of Israel, is the fact, that there is a close artistic affinity and comprehension between these otherwise antipathetic people."[18]

The film shows the Jews, after years of torture, making their way to Poland and pleading for deliverance to King Casimir. An evil count persuades the king to drive them out. The king has meanwhile met a beautiful young Jewess named Esther. They fall in love and when they meet the evil count, he also falls under her charms. The count steals Esther and convinces the king that she has been drowned by her father. The king is thus urged to execute all the Jews as punishment. The night before the massacre, the count throws a feast, alienates his friends, and the king discovers that Esther is still alive. The count is subsequently arrested and executed, King Casimir marries Esther and "Henceforth, there shall be peace for the Jews in Poland."[19]

The *New York Dramatic Mirror* was outraged with the film. "The three-reel piece is marred by continuous exhibition of violence. The scenery between the captions is offensive, and an unpleasant picture is thrown on the screen. . . . the brutality that runs through it chills the heart throbs. . . . Academic reproductions of history's dark pages, at the best are morbid and gloomy theses, and should remain in the dust of the past."[20]

The Universal offered "Jewish" and English advertising material for *Bleeding Hearts* and a version with Yiddish titles.

Goldin's last film for the Universal was a documentary entitled *How the Jews Care for Their Poor*. Announced in late October of 1913, several weeks after the release of *Bleeding Hearts*, it was to show the methods used in caring for the poor through visits to various hospitals and philanthropic societies. It was orginally to be one reel in length,[21] but in December of that year the Universal said it was contributing a two-reel educational picture to the annual banquet of the Brooklyn Federation of Jewish Charities on 21 December. The film, "made especially for the occasion at great expense," would later be released to the theaters.[22] It was favorably received and in April 1914 given a private screening in Manhattan for philanthropists.

The *New York Times* report on the film gives it the appearance of fiction. A young Russian Jewish widow arrives in the United States with her two children. She dies a few weeks later, and her brother promises to care for the two children. He, however, falls ill and is taken to the Jewish Hospital in Brooklyn. The children go to the Brooklyn Hebrew Orphan Asylum. When the brother recovers he finds that the children are well cared for and leaves them at the asylum. Years later, the little orphan boy graduates and gives an address to the Brooklyn Federation of Jewish Charities commending them for all the help they have given his family over the years.[23] There is no record that the film was ever put into general release.

Sidney Goldin went on to work for other independent motion picture companies. In June of 1913, when he was still under contract to the Universal, Ruby Feature Film Company announced that Goldin had directed *The Black 107*. Produced by Lewis J. Rubinstein, *The Black 107* (based on the Black Hundred) was about the activities of this group "in the persecution of the chosen people in Russia."[24] The first trade advertisement for the film appeared in November 1913 and claimed that the film was based on the "Recent Trial in Kiev."[25] It was released in December of that year and features Jan Smoelski, a former revolutionary agent from St. Petersburg. The lower East Side audiences packed the house. "Go to Rivington Street, just east of the Bowery any Sunday after luncheon when there's a racial film on the circuit, if you want to know what a human gorge is," said *Variety* in one of its rare, early film reviews. Still, "The manager at the the Wacco [Theater] must have realized the playlet's artificial texture, for the operator whipped the reels along at a sixty-mile clip."[26] (It was a very common practice to fill out or shorten the length of a film, by either speeding up or slowing down the hand cranking of the projector.) The Chicago police seized *The Black 107* when it was shown at the Keclizie Theatre in

December and the Trans-Oceanic Film Company (probably the States Rights distributor) filed suit in federal court to prevent the restraining order.

Goldin appears once more, in May 1914, as the director/author of *Escaped from Siberia* for the Great Players Feature Film Corporation. In this five-reel feature, he once again uses his favorite theme, a young non-Jew falling in love with a beautiful Jewish maiden, followed by parental disapproval. The girl and her family are banished to Siberia and finally escape to the United States, where they land under the Statue of Liberty. The poor, lovesick young Russian count ultimately joins the Nihilists.[27]

In June of that year (released July), Goldin directed and wrote *Uriel Acosta* from the play by Karl F. Gutzkow, starring Ben Adler and Rosetta Conn. The film ran over an hour, far too long, according to *Variety*. "In Jewish settlements, colonies, or neighborhoods, this picture will excite interest and draw at the box office, otherwise it won't create a ripple."[28]

Two other companies tried for the Jewish audience with films released with Yiddish intertitles. Kalem released *A Passover Miracle* on 30 March 1914, in time for the Passover holidays. It was produced with the assistance of the Bureau of Education of the Jewish Community of New York and starred Henri Leone and Irene Boyle, both Kalem stock players. Shalom Masimon of the Bureau of Education attended the filming in order to ensure the authenticity. The plot harks back to the earlier theme of Jewish films, in which a young immigrant is seduced by the riches of America. Samuel, son of Ratkowitz, is put through medical school by his foster sister and sweetheart Lena. Sam, however, becomes enamored of a flashy stenographer, Rebecca, and is forced to borrow money from Lena to pay for her amusements. Sam becomes ashamed of his family and leaves on graduation night. His father declares that he no longer has a son. When Rebecca finally tires of Sam, the latter returns home. It is Passover Eve, and as Lena opens the door to welcome Elijah, she discovers Sam outside, crying. He is forgiven and the family is reunited.[29]

This film was obviously a novelty for Kalem, a company known for lively adventure films though in earlier days, Kalem had made a name for itself with Christian religious spectacles. As reported in the Kalem house organ, Danny, the property man, had great difficulty in finding a *kittel,* the white shroud worn by Orthodox Jews on the holy days. He finally found one, but it was too short for the actor, who was over six feet. The *kittel* was made for a man of five feet. Danny's response to the problem was to announce: "the only thing that remains to be done is to get a shorter actor!"[30]

The *New York Dramatic Mirror,* one of the few early trade papers that actually reviewed films (most papers depended on company press releases), commended *A Passover Miracle* on its attention to details, but noted that the titles "are in Hebrew and English."[31] Kalem's press releases said they were in Yiddish and English and the Cleveland Jewish paper advertised, "Titles in English and Jewish."[32]

In October 1914, the Box Office Attraction Company (William Fox), announced its entry into the Jewish film market with a version of Israel Zangwill's *The Children of the Ghetto.* Frank Powell directed and Wilton Lackay repeated his stage role as Reb Shemuel (Rabbi Samuel Jacobs in some versions of the film). In this case, it is the father who is deserted by hs children. His son runs away and is killed in a cabaret brawl, the father arriving too late to save him. His daughter runs away with a man and his wife dies. Several years later, Reb Shemuel is sorrowfully performing the Passover seder when his daughter and her two children reappear and the family is reunited.[33] The film was well received both in America and in England.

Until early 1914, Kalem, Universal, and Box Office Attraction Company experimented with courting the Jewish audience with Yiddish advertising and titles on their Jewish melodramas. However, World War I ended these experiments. All production stopped in Poland. In Russia, first the war, then the revolution completely changed the film industry. American films began their domination of the world market. The Jews were to enter a period of great cultural and intellectual life and a bit of calm, at least for a while.

# 3 World War I to the Coming of Sound

Worldwide film production decreased after World War I, and so did the production of Yiddish films. Short films were still being made, as they would always, but the heyday of one- and two-reel films, and the daily changes of bill, had become a thing of the past. Audiences proved that they were capable of long attention, and features changed from being "specials" to the norm. Filmmaking was becoming an even more expensive proposition. Meanwhile, as a country's attitude toward Jews became more lenient and the national film industry prospered, its capacity for catering to minority audiences increased. This trend was especially noticeable in Austria and the new Union of Soviet Socialist Republics.

During the war, Russian Jews fought bravely for the czar and, in the long term, were rewarded in no logical fashion. As German and Austrian troops approached, Jews were evacuated. The Pale was greatly reduced by the German invasion, and this area could no longer accommodate large numbers of Jews. Many evacuees had to be moved to the Russian interior.

Temporarily, Jews were given some privileges such as increased university enrollment. Intellectuals began to champion the cause of Jewish rights, and it was assumed that with the end of the war, Jewish equality would be a necessity for the reconstruction and reorganization of the Russian state.

The Jews welcomed the February Revolution of 1917. Shortly after the czar's abdication, the provisional government published a decree that effectively declared Jews equal citizens of the empire. Lenin included the Jews in the "Declaration of the Rights of Nationalists" issued on 15 November 1917. They were considered a minority that would be allowed to develop their full potential.

But then on 20 October 1918, the Jewish Commissariat passed a resolution banning all "institutions hitherto operating in the Jewish quarter, like the 'communities' and the rest, no longer have any place in our life."[1] As a result, most synagogues were closed, and rabbis and other synagogue officials were placed on a level with other ministers of religion and treated as "declassed" members of society. In 1920, all Zionist organizations (which under Czar Nicholas II had become a potent force in Jewish life, even though underground) were outlawed, along with all recognized Jewish groups (the Bund, People's Party, etc.). The four years after the Revolution also brought with them a new series of pogroms in the Ukraine and White Russia.

In 1921, the Soviet Union reached a certain measure of political stability. The new regime elevated Yiddish to a national language, that of the Jewish minority, and instituted Soviet Jewish schools that had to use Yiddish as their language of instruction. These secular institutions replaced the traditional cheder and yeshiva, though as late as 1927 many of the latter still operated in smaller towns.[2] The schools offered the same curriculum as the general Soviet schools plus one course on Yiddish literature that emphasized communist rather than Jewish criteria. As the years progressed, enrollment in these schools decline.

Until the mid-1930s, literature and theater thrived. The Jewish communist leaders approved of supplying the Yiddish-speaking public with books and periodicals in their own language. Because this was a state-supported venture, the publishing companies did not worry about sales and profits.

Authors received government stipends and if a large number of copies was sold, they obtained additional royalties. Indeed, the volume of work created by Soviet Yiddish writers far outnumbered that of other large communities in the United States and Poland. Much of the literature was made up of Yiddish reprints of ideological speeches, material which proportionately increased in the thirties. The most important branches of Yiddish literature were novels, poetry, and essays in literary history and criticism. Also popular were reprints of the great writers of the past.

Theater also flourished for a time. Habimah, the Hebrew theatrical group, was one of the highlights, but it left the Soviet Union in 1926 when all Hebrew culture was banned. Its place was taken by government-subsidized Yiddish theaters in Jewish centers such as Moscow, Kiev, and Minsk.

Private production continued until 1921 in Moscow, the Ukraine, and the Crimea. Many of the film companies fled to Odessa and Yalta where they were able to continue production. Records show that over 350 privately produced films were made in that period.[3] The only real changes in the films, during these years, was the increase of freedom of choice in source material to include satirical pieces. In 1917 Josef Soifer directed another six-reel version of *The Beilis Case,* which was released after the Revolution. Alexander Arkatov, who had worked for Pathé, made a series of Jewish films in Odessa in 1917, including *The Bloody Jest* from Sholom Aleichem. Arkatov continued in 1918 with *Judge, People,* by I. L. Peretz and *If I Were Rothschild* (Sholom Aleichem). Many other works by Sholom Aleichem were filmed during those years. Then, in 1918 Arkatov fled to Hollywood and Josef Soifer to Paris.

The first Soviet films were being produced late in June of 1918. The "Agit-train," a train traveling the countryside disseminating moral support and carrying, among other sources of propaganda, a film crew, was introduced later that year. These Agit-trains were later to become self-contained film laboratories. Meanwhile, the Cinema Committee contracted with the remaining commercial firms to make films. At a conference in December 1918, government film production was organized and the *agitka*, filmed propaganda, began. One such film, *Comrade Abram*, concerned a Jew, who, after surviving both the imperialist war and the horrors of pogroms, joined the Red Army to defeat the Whites.[4] The films were made basically by the older, more skilled commercial filmmakers, but with young enthusiastic men and women joining them.

As the years passed, young men returned from the front and eagerly joined the new film industry. Most of the pre-Revolution filmmakers fled the country and the Soviet government organized and reorganized the film industry. At the height of Soviet artistic and experimental film production in the twenties, even Jewish topics became more or less commonplace. All of these films, as did Soviet films of the time, conveyed some message to the populace, be it overt propaganda or merely a contrast to things in the past.

The first Jewish film was *Jewish Regiment,* made in 1923, probably with Gregory Gritcher as director.[5] Gritcher worked on another Russian film, assisting Alexis Granowski (Granovsky). For, as manager of the Moscow GOSET (Jewish People's Theatre), the latter wrote and directed an adaption of Sholom Aleichem's *Menachem Mendel* stories in 1925 or 1926. Known both as *Jewish Luck (Yiddishe Glikn)* and *The Matchmaker,* the cast includes Shlomo Mikhoels, Tamara Adelheim as "Beila the bride," and other members of the GOSET. In this adaptation, Menachem Mendel, the *luftmensh*,[6] became a tool of the bourgeoisie and an enemy of the proletariat, but also a victim of the old capitalist order. Mikhoels made Mendel a Chaplinesque figure who leaves home and looses "millions" in his various occupations. He is undone when, as a matchmaker he mistakenly arranges a marriage between two girls. The film was well received in Moscow but not released in the United States until 1935 and then with a sound track. Advertised as "[a] Jewish Talking Picture with a cast of 500 artists,"[7] it was Granowski's only Russian film. When GOSET toured Eastern Europe in 1926, Granowski chose not to return to Russia. He went on to direct a few films in Europe and the United States, most notably *Moscow Nights,* 1938.

The Moscow Habimah also appeared in a film when, in 1926, several members of the company were invited by Sovkino to work on an adaptation of Sholom Aleichem's *The Deluge,* entitled *Mabul.* The rights for the actor's film participation was purchased from the collective, thus no single person received a salary, the money being divided among the group, whether or not particular individuals had taken part in the film. This was also part of Habimah's antistar attitude.

To the actors, film was a new experience. They put in an appearance only when they were needed. Sovkino had also decided that they would have no say in the creative aspects of the film. To add to the confusion, the director, Yevgeni Ivanov-Barkov, had never directed a film, and his theater experience was limited. His unidentified assistant, however, had once owned a private film studio and so it was he, who set the tone of the film, insisting on absolute realism. The film dealt with life in a small Jewish town during czarist times. It centered on a familiar topic in pre-Soviet films: the fight of the Jewish intelligentsia against the Black Hundred terrorists.

Leningrad, the city in which *Mabul* was filmed, was scoured for props like Torah scrolls, embroidered velvet covers, and prayer books for a synagogue scene. Real Cossacks with their horses, soldiers, and general riffraff were hired for the pogroms. The assistant's briefing centered on total realism—the need to have the audience shudder. The Cossacks were to beat a group of Russian extras, dressed as Jews with prayer shawls, phylacteries, beards, and earlocks. When the assistant director gave the word, the Cossacks followed his command quite literally, not even stopping when instructed. From then on, the Russian extras refused to act in mass scenes or to wear beards.[8]

Both Ivanov-Barkov and his assistant were removed from the film and replaced. Their successor failed to finish the film, and Boris Illyitch Vershilov, who directed *The Golem* for Habimah, became the third to try. In 1927, wind of a scandal in the Soviet film industry reached the United States. Some fifty former directors and other prominent members of Goskino, Proletkino, and Cultkino were arrested and brought to trial in an investigation of waste of money. One of the prominent films mentioned was *Mabel* [sic]. The producer had spent money on rewriting the screenplay and had filmed the picture four times, spending $100,000 for no result.[9] Habimah claimed they never saw the film.

Soviet films also made use of the contemporary Russian Jewish writers, especially Isaac Babel. Babel intellectually supported the Communist regime and wrote several screenplays, most of which were never produced for ideological reasons. Babel himself fell out of favor with the government and disappeared in the 1930s. He was executed, and years later the government admitted its mistake. In the 1920s, however, Babel was a much-admired writer, two of whose screenplays were based on Yiddish literature.

The first was from his own work, *The Odessa Tales*. *Benya Krik (The Jewish Gangster)*, made in 1926, was based on several of these tales and was rewritten numerous times. In the final version, Benya Krik goes over to the side of the Communists during the Revolution. The Red Army commander invites the criminal leader to dinner and shoots him in the back. The film was banned because of official displeasure with the ending. It was released six months after completion in January 1927.[10] The director, Vladimir Vilner, later directed a version of *Motel The Weaver*.

Part of the scenario for *Wandering Stars*, Babel's second screenplay, adapted from Sholom Aleichem's stories, remains. It tells how a young Jewess, Rachel Monko, comes to Moscow to enter the Moscow Higher Women's Course. She is refused lodging in a Russian rooming house because of her Jewishness. She pairs off with a young radical in order to sleep in a hotel for prostitutes and their customers. There the fragment ends.[11] Critics regarding the 1926 film, directed by Gregory Gritcher, as "decadent and ideologically deficient."[12]

Babel also wrote *The Chinese Mill* (probably from Upton Sinclair's *Jimmy Higgins*) in 1928, and rewrote *Pilots*. He

Poster for American release (1933) of *Laughter through Tears*. The Yiddish title is, *Motel Peyse, the Cantor's Son*. (Rutenberg & Everett Yiddish Film Library of the American Jewish Historical Society)

formulated one of the revisions for Eisenstein's *Bezhin Meadow* and worked on a script of Nikolai Alexayevich Ostrowsky's *How the Steel Was Tempered.*

Sholom Aleichem stories continued to be a popular basis for screenplays (perhaps due to the writer's slightly cynical point of view), as in *Laughter through Tears* of 1928. This film continued in the tradition of Olga Preobrazhenskaya's *Peasant Women of Ryazan* of 1927 portraying the past without any overt propaganda to emphasize the glories of the Revolution. Three tales, set in a *shtetl*, are interwoven to present an entertaining film and a portrayal of the unbelievable poverty and desperation of pre-Revolution Jews. Among the stories are the get-rich-quick scheme of two young men cornering the ink market and the machinations of Motele the cantor's son. The film was directed by Gritcher for Vufku in the Ukraine. Not released in the United States until 1933, it was shown with an added Yiddish narration track by Michael Rosenberg and the Yiddish Art Theatre.

Not all the Yiddish films were based on existing literature. In a foreshadowing of the films to be made under the tighter restrictions of the thirties, three films came from Russian sources: *Seeds of Freedom* in 1927, *Cain and Artem* in 1929, and *A Jew at War*, dated 1931 but probably made earlier. These were all filmed as silents and released abroad with synchronized music tracks.

Grigori Roshal, who directed for the Habimah, entered cinema in 1925 with *The Skotinins*. *Seeds of Freedom* was his second film, written with his codirector and later wife Vera Stroyeva. Leonid M. Leonidoff stars as a provincial governor and an orthodox rabbi. Hirsh Lekkert (referred to as the Jewish fighter and played by J. Undershalk) is the ringleader in a Jewish rebellion against the harsh governor.[13]

Roshal's next Yiddish film, *A Jew at War*, again centered on a fighting Jew's rebellion against the czarist regime. Venyamin Zuskin of the Moscow Jewish Art Theatre played David Gorelick, a young Jewish soldier in World War I, who struggles in the trenches with a German soldier only to discover that they were friends before the war. Gorelick fights in the

Revolution and as reward for valor is appointed manager of a shoe factory. Treachery once more prevails when, adhering to the goals of the Revolution, workers who demanded special privileges stab him in the back. It is the end of Gorelick but not of the Revolution.[14]

Between the wars, Poland, as an independent country, flourished. Until the Nazi invasion, Polish Jewry, Jewish culture and the arts in general flowered. With the defeat of the Central Powers, a free Polish government was established in Lublin, on 7 November 1918. Ignacy Daszynkski proclaimed full political and civic equality for all citizens. Joseph Pilsudski became head of state and invited representatives of the Jewish community to attend a conference to help organize the new Polish government. Unfortunately, this was not to last. The Russo-Polish War (1920–21) directly affected the lives of two million out of a total of about three million Jews in Poland in 1919. The Poles accused the Jews of sympathizing with the Russians, and the Russian accused the Jews of sympathizing with the Poles. Over a thousand pogroms were instigated between December 1920 and April 1921. Then came the constitution of March 1921—one of the most democratic of postwar Europe. All citizens were equal and eligible for public office. Theoretically, Jews were no longer second-class citizens. But the constitution was never properly enforced.[15]

The government failed to protect Jewish life and property, and the economic status of the Jews declined. Yet, despite a continual worsening of the Jewish plight, Jewish cultural life flourished. The postwar independent Poland became the center for Yiddish letters. The major older authors, I. L. Peretz, Sholom Aleichem, Mendele Mocher Seforim, and S. Anski had died after the war, and the new writers were now experimenting with form. Two major Yiddish publishing houses were established. By 1939, there were 27 daily Jewish newspapers, over 100 weeklies, 58 monthlies, 4 bimonthlies, 17 biannual yearbooks; 391 publications in all, of which 70 percent were in Yiddish.[16]

Yiddish theater also continued, despite the gradually worsening economic conditions. In the 1920s and 1930s, there was hardly a town without at least an amateur Yiddish theater company. In 1926, Zygmund Turkow and Ida Kaminska formed the Warsaw Yiddish Art Theater with a wide repertory. The Vilna Troupe continued to perform and tour. Guest artists came from New York, and the Moscow Jewish Art Theater also toured throughout Eastern Europe.

The twenties and thirties were also vintage years for the Polish film industry. In 1919, the first year of freedom, 22 movies were produced. This level was maintained until the introduction of sound films.

Leo-Forbert Films, working with the Polish nationalistic company, Leo Films, made three features based on Yiddish literature or theater. The photographer, Henryk Bojm, who worked for Forbert, together with cameraman Seweryn Steinwurcel, Forbert's cousin, convinced Zygmund Turkow to film his version of *Tkijes Khaf*. The film was to be financed by advances from theaters. Turkow, perhaps remembering the problems in the prewar films, agreed provided a good director were brought in from the outside. Bojm promised him a foreign director, but on the first day of filming no director had been hired. Turkow took over the production. He filmed exteriors in Vilna and Warsaw and also played the prophet Elijah who makes good the vow of two Talmud students that their children should marry. Bojm at first prepared Polish intertitles but realizing the possibilities of further commercial gain, added Yiddish ones.[17]

The following year, Leo Forbert, Henryk Bojm, and Serweryn Steinwurzel produced *Jeden Z 36 (Der Lamedvovnik, One of the 36)*. They hired Henry Szaro to direct and retained Steinwurzel for camera. It starred Jonas Turkow.

In the last year before sound film came to Poland, Forbert Films made [*In the*] *Polish Woods (W Lasach Polskich)*. Henryk Bojm once again wrote the scenario from the novel by Joseph Opatoshu. Jonas Turkow directed. It starred Dina Blumenfeld as Rachel and Silven Rich as Mordechai. Interiors were shot in the studio in Warsaw and exteriors at Kotzk. Forbert screened the completed film for Agudath Israel, the orthodox group. They protested several scenes, such as a shot of an unmarried man and woman kissing and one of a man and woman approaching the rabbi's house. The film was cut to conform with their wishes.

In 1918 there were 300,000 Jews living in Austria with 200,000 of them living in Vienna. The Treaty of St. Germain in 1919 had guaranteed Jewish minority rights, but as usual the various Jewish groups disagreed on the interpretation of this treaty. The government in no way enforced Jewish rights. Attempts were made to segregate Jews in schools and universities, deprive the voting rights of Jews who had settled in Austria after the war, and deprive war refugees of citizenship. Between the wars a number of Jewish schools and Hebrew classes were founded and there was strong support for Zionist movements.

As in most European countries, the Austrian national cinema dates back to the beginning of the twentieth century. From 1918 to 1922, Austrian films boomed. In 1917, 38 films were made in Austria. In 1920, the peak year of production, 142 films were made.[18] Otto Kreisler made two "Jewish" films during this period, *Theodor Herzl der Bannerträger (Theodore Herzl, the Banner Carrier)* and *Die Juden von Toledo (The Jews of Toledo)*. His last film on a Jewish topic was made in 1921. This was the one-reel film for Helio-Film or Ekran films entitled *Das Judenmädel (The Jewish Girl)*. It starred Molly Picon and Ferdinand Bonn and concerned the adventures of a Jewish girl in Russia.

Meanwhile, Sidney Goldin, who had been director of the Eclair Studios in Paris, moved in 1921 to Vienna and formed his own company, Goldin Films. At the same time, Molly Picon and her husband Jacob Kalich were touring Europe and stopped several times in Vienna. Three of the films Goldin directed at this time were just melodramas, *Ihre Vergangenheit (Her Past)*, *Führe Uns Nicht in Versuchung (Lead Us Not into Temptation)* and *Hütet Eure Töchter (Protect Your Daughters)*, the last with Molly Picon and Sybille de Bree.

Later, in 1923, Goldin and Picon made *Ost und West (East*

*and West,)* for Listo Films (a major Austrian production company). The film shows an American bringing his daughter to Poland. As a joke, she stages a mock marriage with a yeshiva *bocher,* (played by Jacob Kalich,) but the marriage is legitimatized as the young man places a ring on her finger. "It was a very well-made film because they did good work in Vienna in the silent film," said the star, Molly Picon.[19] It was released in New York by Kerman Films under the title *Mazel Tov.* The American version totaled eight reels and played at a special showing for ten days with Yiddish intertitles.[20]

Maurice Schwartz's company toured Europe and when they passed through Vienna in 1924, Goldin directed them in *Yiskor (Thou Shalt Remember)* for Jüdische-Kunstfilm. In it, Schwartz played Leybke, a young Jewish forester who becomes a hunter for the duke and refuses the advances of the duke's daughter. He is tortured in the Ukrainian bear dance, when, dressed in a bear skin, he is whipped and killed. The film appears to have been shown in the United States. Goldin then left Vienna and does not resurface until 1929.

Yiddish culture in America reached its peak in the twenties. During the war years, the immigrant Jews had prospered, so money was available to invest in the twenty Yiddish theaters in New York. Young actors were entering the theater and beginning to take over the major roles, and playwrights had come over from Europe. All through the twenties and thirties American critics saw the Yiddish theater as a model of innovation and accomplishment. Yiddish literature for a time also flourished. In the early twenties, there were Yiddish dailies in all the major cities in the United States and Canada. The *Forward* of New York alone had a daily circulation of 200,000.

While Austria, the Soviet Union, and Poland's film industries were thriving both artistically and financially in the 1920s, so did the American film, in Hollywood. New York City, which had supplied the audience and actors for Jewish films, was no longer the center of film production in the United States. The Hollywood studio system was now entrenched (with corporate offices remaining in the East) and the independents of 1914 were now the major studios of the 1920s. Sound was introduced in 1926 with *Don Juan* and then *The Jazz Singer* in 1927, and before the end of the decade, the silents were gone.

But for some reason, Hollywood abandoned the Jewish immigrant population. Productions had become larger and changes of theatrical bill less frequent. The Jews had their own cultural outlets, but this did not seem to include films.

*The Jews in Poland*, released in 1920, helped to ease the memories and some of the pain of immigration. Produced by the Jewish Picture Corporation, it is a travelogue of the Polish *shtetls*. The scenes, not linked by any plot, include market places and townspeople of Brest-Litovsk and Pinsk where a pogrom had recently taken place.[21]

Louis N. Jaffe formed Jaffe Art Films in an attempt to fill the gap created by Hollywood's lack of interest in the Jewish audience. The company's policy was "to present the Jew as he is done in plays, done in an artistic manner."[22] The cast of *Broken Hearts*, released 1926, reads like a program for Maurice Schwartz's popular Jewish Art Theatre: Schwartz, who also directed, Wolf Goldfadden, Isidor Cashier, Anna Appel, Julius Adler, and Lila Lee (a popular actress). Schwartz played the part of a young Russian immigrant, Benjamin, who flees his homeland when the czarist government finds his writings treasonable. He learns that the wife he left behind has died in a massacre and so marries Ruth, a cantor's daughter. On hearing that his wife is still alive, Ruth persuades Benjamin to return to Russia. But while he is travelling, his wife dies in a government hospital. So Benjamin returns home only to discover that Ruth has disappeared. He finds her in her father's house on Yom Kippur.

Reviews were generally favorable for the story and acting, the former so reminiscent of the early Victor films. Technically, the film is considered very slow moving, with a tendency to dwell on the tragic aspects of the story.[23] No other films appeared under the Jaffe Art Film banner perhaps because the introduction of the sound film and the increasing technical difficulty of film production prevented Louis N. Jaffe from reaching the goals he set forth.

The era of the silent film had come to a close, and the European and American film industry were busy learning how to cope with the new technology. After the artistic and technical peak of the mid-twenties, worldwide film business would have to adapt to a sudden change.

This period of production created memorable films. The revitalized and reorganized post-Revolution Soviet film industry actively courted its Jewish audience. From 1917 to 1924, Yiddish culture thrived and this was reflected, briefly, in some of the films of that period, with innovative adaptations of classic Yiddish authors like Sholom Aleichem and newer ones like Isaac Babel. Poland also had its brief spotlight with Leo-Forbert Films trying its hand at Yiddish literature. Austrian film blossomed and Sidney Goldin settled there in 1921 to film. Only in the United States were the Jews ignored in the popular culture of film. But they had the Yiddish theater at its prime to console and satisfy the immigrants' desire for Yiddish art.

# 4   1929–1934: The Yiddish Talkie

Until 1929, there were no real Yiddish films—none that literally spoke to their audience in Yiddish. But with the coming of sound film, the Yiddish-speaking Jews found a new form of entertainment that rivaled the Yiddish theater and, as the theater declined, preserved its memories.

The depression arrived and with it the condition of Jews in Europe continued to deteriorate. Only now it became more and more difficult to emigrate. In contrast, the Jews who had immigrated to America were already becoming assimilated. The first movement out of the ghetto, if only to the Bronx and Brooklyn, was taking place from the Lower East Side. Jewish communities outside New York City were publishing local weeklies in English and Yiddish and keenly feeling their isolation from a larger, more vital Jewish community.

In 1930, the *Telegraph* gloated that New York was the center of just about everything, thus it was with good reason that Warner Brothers launched its Spanish-language productions there. Then followed some talk of German theater actors dubbing silent films in German and the last paragraph mentioned a small company called Judea Films. The *Telegraph* predicted that New York City would become a center of foreign-language film production, especially in the case of Yiddish, as there were scores of good Yiddish actors in New York.[1]

New York never really became a center for foreign-language productions, not in a way that would ever compete with Hollywood's film output or that of any film-producing European country. It did, for a while, however, dominate the genre of the Yiddish-language films. In all, over a period of a decade, some fifty of these were filmed—hardly the "boom" *Variety* claimed in 1940, the last year of production.[2]

To speak of the American Yiddish film is to speak of Joseph Seiden—and Joe would have agreed. Singlehandedly, Seiden started regular production of Yiddish language films, feeding the market that he himself had probably created. Seiden was an opportunist who had no pretentions about the quality of the films he produced, and he was just as willing to film a "race" picture such as *Paradise in Harlem* as a classic of the Yiddish stage. Born in 1892, of an Austrian father, he spent his life working in motion pictures. He was the official photographer for the Baltic Mission of the American Relief Expedition in 1919 and worked as a cameraman for Universal on *Uncle Tom's Cabin* in Plattsburg, New York. In the twenties he was the boxing cameraman with his own firm, Seiden Films. He filmed the Dempsey-Tunney fight and later worked with Sidney Goldin.

Seiden teamed up with Ivan Abramson, an early director and producer, to produce a series of silent Yiddish newsreels. The first "issue" was a luncheon of the building committee of the Yeshiva College of America. According to Seiden:

> I was hand cranking my Pathé Camera and Judge Rosolsk had just presented the first speaker Harry Fishel. Before my camera lens stepped Mr. Fishel, who without further ado said in far from perfect English, "I donate one hundred thousand dollars." Well! never before or since have I lost control at a camera, but at that nonchalant donation I slowed up my steady grind in astonishment. I quickly picked up as Mr. Fishel sat down and Nathan Lamport took his place and he too made the same donation.[3]

The success of these newsreels, along with the coming of sound, led Seiden to attempt Yiddish talkies. "That there are millions of Jewish film fans who would support product in their own tongues is given by organizers as the underlying reason for the formation of Judea Pictures Corporation." It was incorporated in December 1929, with Joseph Seiden as president, Sam Berliner as secretary and treasurer, and Moe Goldman, owner of four Bronx picture houses, general manager. "[The] company is depending upon Goldman to exercise the same ingenuity in production that he has in exhibiting: Moe, it will be recalled, is the lad who cheated the electrics by talking for the male screen players and getting his femme cashier to speak for the women."[4] An auspicious beginning. They announced four shorts, budgeted at $15,000 each. Following would be a special on Zion history, shot in Palestine. In all, twenty-six "talkers" were announced as the original production goal. Seiden set his sights on 250 theaters in key cities that were known to have a large Jewish draw. Not taking any chances, Seiden continued such productions as puppet films and his film equipment rental company.

Production started in February 1930, and three weeks later the first two shorts, *Style and Class* and *The Shoemaker's Romance,* were ready. On 19 March they were playing at the R.K.O. Tilyou Theater in Coney Island. In early April five Fox Theaters in Brooklyn booked them. Judea Films, from their headquarters at 727 Seventh Avenue, offered such advertising material as silent trailers, 8 × 10 photos, and one-sheets, free of charge. Theater owners were encouraged to sell the two-reel shorts as features.

It was all very presumptuous of Seiden with shorts budgeted at $3,000 each, not the announced $15,000. With this small amount of money to spend, there was no room for error. The actors, all Yiddish theater professionals such as Joseph Buloff, Leah Noemi, Marty Baratz, and Goldie Eisman, were rehearsed extensively, for they were allowed only one take. Once a scene had started, it had to run for the full ten minutes of the sixteen-inch recording disc. Being stage actors, they rarely muffed their lines, but if they did, it appeared on the finished film. Seiden had rented the Scenic Studio on Thirty-Eighth Street[5], some phonograph recording equipment, and several old Klieg incandescent stage lights.

The walls were padded with monks' cloth for soundproofing. The rule was simply to "pump in all the light you had."[6] Two cameras were used, one being run by Seiden himself, and both were inside sound-proofed booths on wheels. The first camera shot the entire set while the second took in close-ups and the central action. Sidney Goldin directed. All the early shorts and features were shot this way.

In April, the first feature, *My Yiddishe Mama (Mine Yiddishe Mame)*, lasting sixty minutes, and starring Mae Simon, was completed. It began with a prologue that referred to Abraham and Isaac, and stressed the desirability of honoring one's parents, especially mothers who sacrifice their lives for their children. The story opens with a surprise birthday party for Eddie Rabinowitz, given by his parents, David and Mae, and by his brother Seymour and sister Helen. Later, David is killed, so Mae must go to work. Eddie Stein leads Helen astray and Seymour spends his mother's money. When years later, Seymour, now a prominent lawyer, hears of a woman abandoned by her children, he agrees to force them to support her. He is introduced to his own mother. Mae forgives them, the family is reunited and the picture ends happily.[7]

*My Yiddishe Mama* was released in May 1930. It brought a storm of protest from the Hebrew Actors Union, the representative body of all Yiddish stage actors. A resolution was passed prohibiting members of the union from appearing in the new Yiddish talkies. Union representatives stated that these talkies were injurious to the reputation of the Yiddish theater and also employed nonunion actors who had no theatrical experience. Adding to these grievances, Reuben Guskin, the union manager, pointed out that the films were only being shown in neighborhoods where there were already Yiddish theaters. The Jewish public, he claimed, was being misled into believing that the actors would appear personally in the theaters where the films were being shown.[8] It is doubtful that the actors, unemployed several months each year, would have obeyed anyway, but Seiden managed to convince the union leaders that the films would help rather than hinder their craft, and so the resolution was dropped.

## 1929–1934: THE YIDDISH TALKIE

All through this, Seiden continued announcing plans. Mildred Block, Jennie Goldstein, and Bella Gudinsky were being signed to long-term contracts. An adaptation of Tolstoy's *The Living Corpse* was planned with Samuel Goldenberg, Sadell Epstein, and Louis Weisberg.[9] More shorts were shot and in May he was making plans for a chain of Yiddish talkie theaters, with one at Second Avenue and Eighth Street, in the heart of the Yiddish theater district; and one in Brighton Beach and Prospect Avenue, the Bronx. He would then expand nationwide. Judea Films would provide a weekly change of bill. But by the end of August negotiations had not yet been completed. Seiden still talked about a new feature and five shorts each month but the deal was never finalized, and he continued to have distribution problems throughout the early years of production.

Seiden sent Moe Goldman to Europe to establish distribution bases in England, Poland, and other centers of Jewish life. When Goldman returned, Rivling and Company of Tel Aviv offered to purchase *My Yiddishe Mama* for Palestine and Syria. The deal was closed and the prints shipped. When the film premiered on 27 September 1930, the audience became enraged. Some spattered the screen with ink while others left the theater in a demonstrative fashion and were greeted with cheers by the crowd outside. The British police were called in to aid the local police. People felt that Yiddish endangered the Hebrew language, so Vice-Mayor Rokeach prohibited a second showing of the film. A compromise between the municipal officials and Judea Films resulted in the talking and singing parts of the film being cut.[10] Not until after World War II would a Yiddish talkie be shown in Israel.

Undaunted by this loss of potential market, Judea Films continued production. *The Living Corpse* was dropped and *Eternal Fools,* a somber domestic drama with Yudel Dubinsky followed, but did very poor business. At the end of 1930, Seiden's "special," *The Voice of Israel* was ready. Featuring the best-known cantors of the day, the cast included Yossele Rosenblatt, Meyer Machtenburg and his choir, and Cantor Leibele Waldman. Produced on a budget of $20,000, it contained historical scenes from various silent biblical films. These were narrated in English and tied together by relevant hymns sung by the cantors. The films received good critical notices but failed to attract an audience.[11] As most of the profits from the earlier films were used to finance this epic, Goldman and Berliner chose this time to sell their interest in Judea to Seiden. From then on, Seiden was going to play it safe and give the audience exactly what it wanted.

By 1931, Judea Films was boasting "Yiddish Talking Pictures, proved business builders . . . nineteen are ready now."[12] These included his three features, *Eternal Fools, My Yiddishe Mama,* and *Shulamith,* seven one-reel shorts, and nine two-reel shorts. Titles of the latter included *Kol Nidre I & II, Broken Doll, Jewish Melody,* and *Jewish Gypsy.* They were written by Sholem Secunda, Isidore Lillian, Seymour Reichtzeit, Abraham Raizin, and others and starred Hymie Jacobson, Menasha Skulnick, Marty Baratz, and Cantor Leibele Waldman. They ranged from comic sketches to pious cantorials. In all, from 1930 to 1931, Seiden made some nineteen shorts. All were directed by Sidney Goldin, and described by Seiden as "tearjerkers all."[13]

Though Seiden did not have an efficient distribution system, his first (and subsequent) films played for several years. In the New York City area he was able to find theaters for his films soon after their completion. *Eternal Fools* played in Philadelphia in September 1930, but *My Yiddishe Mama,* completed first, did not reach the city's Metropolitan Opera House until October of that year, after it had played abroad. It was not until April 1931 that *My Yiddishe Mama* found a theater in Cleveland, and then it was only for three days. Ten days later, between April 15 and 17, it played at the Ritz and from April 22 to 24, at the Waldorf. Due to the efficiency of the Jewish Telegraphic Agency, *The Scribe,* the Jewish weekly of Portland, Oregon, announced on 12 September 1930, "First Yiddish All Talking Picture Given Preview." This article referred to *Eternal Fools,*[14] yet none of Seiden's films played in Portland throughout the entire decade. Later in

Poster for *East Side Sadie*, one of the first American Yiddish talking pictures, really a silent film with added talking sequences. The poster claims, "It took a year's time to produce" and calls it a "$100,000 production." From the very beginning, the producers made outlandish claims for the quality of their productions. The photographs show the stars: Abe Sinkoff, Mark Schweid, and Boris Rosenthal. (Rutenberg & Everett Yiddish Film Library of the American Jewish Historicall Society)

December 1931, *My Yiddishe Mama* and *The Voice of Israel* played in Detroit, for three days apiece. *The Voice of Israel* did not reach Cleveland until February 1932.

Seiden, with his flamboyant manner and ability to use the Jewish Telegraphic Agency hides one minor fact. He was not the only producer of Yiddish films in the early thirties, and his were not even the first such films. It is hardly a surprise that Seiden borrowed his invention. *East Side Sadie*, a silent film with added talking sequences, was first shown in New York on 20 May 1929, nine months before Seiden began production on his first shorts. As a film, it is scarcely a milestone in quality. *Film Daily* called it "[an] amateurish effort made with a sweatshop atmosphere—rates too poor to merit any rating" and gave it a sarcastic review.[15] Sound sequences included children singing, a cantor singing a wedding prayer, and shouting during a wedding. These were all in Yiddish. Directed by Sidney Goldin, it starred Bertina Goldin, Jack Ellis, and Boris Rosenthal. World Art Film Company, whose name appears on many of the later Polish Yiddish films, was the distributor.

*The Eternal Prayer*, also from 1929, is a true talkie. Again Sidney Goldin directed. It starred Lucy Levin, Anna Appel, and "Schmulikel," the boy cantor. Produced by Metropolitan Studios, sound on disc, it was only a series of Hebrew songs yet this was sufficient for it to be advertised as "First All-Talking Jewish Picture" when it ran in Detroit in December 1929[16] "It is about the worst film ever made, indicating absolutely no knowledge of the cinema, even the most elementary, on the part of the makers. It is a succession of 'acts' with groups keening and singing Hebrew ritual songs, Kaddish, and others. The 'acts' are actually separated by blank intervals."[17]

*The Detroit Jewish Chronicle* of 4 April 1930 ran an article on *Joseph and His Brethren*, "the first Jewish talking picture in the world." It is described as a "spectacular talkie" with a "traditional air" used as a theme song. A Mr. Adolph Gartner is praised for his directorial ability.[18] Nothing else is men-

Rather than worry about the famous egos of the Yiddish theater actors and actresses, it was easier to have everyone's photograph on the poster. *Zein Weibs Lubovnik,* 1931, an early contemporary comedy. (Rutenberg & Everett Yiddish Film Library of the American Jewish Historical Society)

tioned. The film is probably a dubbed silent movie with Yiddish dialogue added.

As Seiden continued to struggle to make Yiddish talkies, other companies tried their hand. Sidney Goldin directed *Zein Weibs Lubovnik (His Wife's Lover)*, for Nathan Hirsh and Morris Kleinerman's High Art Picture Corporation. It was taken from Molnar's *The Guardsman*, fashioned into a play and then brought to the screen by S. R. Simkhof. Billed as the "first Jewish musical comedy talking picture ,"[19] it appears to have been well received and presented a screen novelty—a Yiddish-speaking black maid.

Asher Chasin, who claimed to be director of Seiden's *The Voice of Israel*, tried to cash in on the publicity for that film. He attempted to raise $17,000 for a Yiddish-English talkie, *Kaddish*. It was to be the history of the Joint Distribution Committee worked around the silent film, *The Destruction of Jerusalem*. His novel methods of raising money included the selling of shares of the corporation, and the giving of lessons at $1 per lesson to train people for the production and staging of the film. If these failed, he prepared to found a large organization with a large membership and raise funds. The film was never made, but others managed to complete just this type of film.

Silent films of varying vintages and quality were discovered to be an easy way of producing a Yiddish talking "spectacular." Seiden's *Voice of Israel* and Gartner's *Joseph and His Brethren* were the first. Joseph Green, who later produced his own films in Poland, worked on one of the other early ones. Born in 1905, Joseph Green, originally Greenberg, began his career as an actor on the Yiddish stage. He came to America from Poland with the Vilna Troupe when they introduced *The Dybbuk* in 1923. Two years later, he left the troupe and joined Rudolph and Joseph Schildkraut. When they departed for Hollywood to film *King of Kings*, Green followed them and for several years played small parts in films. He later returned to New York and joined Unzer Theater ("our theater") and then spent four years with Maurice Schwartz's Jewish Art Theater.

In 1931, Green was approached by a man who told him, "The time is ripe for Jewish stuff [films]."[20] (The man may have been Mortimer D. Sikawitt or Samuel Goldstein, both of whose names are on the copyright material.) The plan was to get an Italian silent film, *Joseph in the Land of Egypt,* dub in Yiddish dialogue, and make it a Yiddish talkie. Green agreed to play the part of Joseph. The eighty-minute film, released in 1932, hid its Italian origins. The producer never said that it was anything but a biblical epic, partially filmed in Egypt, and starring members of the Yiddish theater.

Green was paid for his work with a copy of *Joseph.* When he performed in Canada, he brought along the print. In Toronto, Green screened the print for an exhibitor. Though the man spoke no Yiddish he was enthusiastic about the film, and Green signed a contract. "The first week I got out of the film, more than I got the whole year in the theater. . . . That film played quite a few weeks over there and I see that this is a matter to be pursued."[21] He notified the Hebrew Actors Union that he was going out on a sabbatical and took the print to Montreal. The film did even better there.

"All of a sudden, I find myself with a lot of money here. The film business, it hit me, I just had to pursue it."[22]

In order to raise more money, Green returned to New York and organized a cooperative theater. After a year's run of *The Golem,* he traveled as an actor to Lemberg, Poland, and naturally brought along his print of *Joseph in the Land of Egypt.* In Warsaw he found two Jewish theater owners who had a theater between the Jewish and Gentile neighborhoods. At 11:00 P.M. after the last show, they screened the print. The owners wouldn't let him go home without a contract, for in Poland, with three-and-a-half million Jews, there had never been a Yiddish talkie.

Some Jews later approached Green and asked him not to show the film. They were afraid that the Poles' anti-Semitism would cause problems in the Jewish community. On the contrary, the Poles did not care as this was a Jewish film and the Jews were not competing with Polish films.

*Joseph* played all over Poland. Green, knowing little about movies, had only one print. One night, a man approached him during the showing and asked, "Mr. Green, have you got the negative? What are you going to do if something happens to that print? You're out of the business." That night the man, who owned a laboratory, made a negative. In the morning the print was saved.[23]

Few of these early films are as well documented as this one, but the stories behind these dubbed silent films are probably similar.

Adolph and Jennie Gartner appear once again as stars of the "First Yiddish Biblical Talking Picture Produced," *The Sacrifice of Isaac*, screened in Des Moines, Iowa, in November 1932 and also in Chicago and Cleveland. The film is described as having a cast of ten thousand, a five-hundred-voice choir, and a one-hundred-person orchestra.[24] Screenings were always accompanied by special guest appearances of the stars.

Joseph Green and Jacob Mestel participated in the dubbing of a Polish silent film. Actors from the New York Yiddish theater sat around and told a tale of a "fallen woman" as played by the Vilna Troupe, in *A Daughter of Her People*. Jacob Mestel again played the part of the narrator in *A Vilna Legend*, 1933. George Roland directed the new sequences of five men sitting around a table telling the story of thwarted lovers, *Tkijes Khaf*, the 1924 Polish film. Joe Seiden once more got into the act with two of these films. Seiden rereleased the silent Schwartz melodrama *Broken Hearts* as *The Unfortunate Bride of Suffolk Street*. He took the silent, *A Story of the Bible*, added talking scenes of a rabbi teaching his yeshiva students and released it as both *The Eternal Jew* and *Avram Ovenu (Father Abraham)*.

Another little-remembered genre is the Palestine picture, essentially a travelogue with added narration or songs. The Palestine-American Film Company presented *The Dream of My People* in 1933, exploiting the morbid publicity of this being Cantor Josef Rosenblatt's last-recorded songs, since he had died while making the film. From Palestine itself came *Land of Promise (Chayyim Chadasm)*, a forty-five-minute

A late publicity photograph for *The Eternal Jew*, 1931, later retitled *Avram Ovenu*. This was a silent film with added Yiddish narration. Joseph Seiden often retitled and rereleased his films several years after their original release. (Rutenberg & Everett Yiddish Film Library of the American Jewish Historical Society)

Alexander Ford's *Chalutzim*, 1934, possibly the first talking picture made in Palestine. It chronicled the hardships of the early settlers and featured all nonprofessionals. It is a forerunner of the Goskinds' *Mr. Kumen On* and one of a number of pictures celebrating the settlement of Palestine. (Rutenberg & Everett Yiddish Film Library of the American Jewish Historical Society)

production in English made by the Jewish National Fund for publicity purposes. There was also a shorter production under the same title from the Urim Palestine Film Company.

*The Voice of Israel*, no matter how doubtful the end results, was not the only attempt at serious drama and filmmaking by the early Yiddish talkie producers. Maurice Schwartz made his first venture into sound with a version of Sholem Asch's *Uncle Moses*, the tale of a benevolent-despot sweatshop boss and his workers' ultimate success in bringing in a union. *Uncle Moses*, managed, unlike many, to be shown in England in 1938, six years after its production in America.

*The Wandering Jew*, 1933, is another rarity: the only American Yiddish film to comment on the Jewish plight in Germany. It was released by Jewish American Film Art, Inc. which gathered a crew that worked on many other films, experts including George Roland, director and Frank Zukor and J. Bergi Cotner, cameramen. Jacob Mestel wrote the original screenplay and was credited as its adapter and dialoguer. He also starred with Jacob Ben-Ami, who played a great Jewish painter faced with anti-Semitism when his painting of the Wandering Jew is rejected by the Berlin Academy of Art. As he is about to destroy his own canvas, the painting comes to life and the history of the persecution of the Jews is recounted. "They spend money freely if one must judge by the lavish sets and innumerable mob scenes that cover the various historical periods."[25] One can assume that this footage was borrowed from other sources in the usual interest in economy but the few remaining stills of the film show stylish modern sets and a darkly suited Ben-Ami. The film was rereleased in 1938 as *A Jew in Exile* when America was more knowledgeable about the plight of the German Jews.

To supplement the first Yiddish American films, a trickle of Jewish films arrived in the United States via Amkino, the combined distribution arm of the Soviet Film Studios. Those that were shown here were remnants of the experiments of the twenties and the new hardline propaganda films featuring the social realism that was now the policy of the government. The condition of the Jews in the Soviet Union had continued in a steady decline. Culturally, attrition was accelerated by increases in antireligious legislation and propaganda. Eleven Yiddish theaters existed in the Ukraine in 1933, but by 1937 there were four, and a total of twelve in the entire country.

By 1929, the Soviets were using sound. Yiddish, however, was no longer a language in favor and it was used to further the scope of the film's audience. Only two Yiddish talkies of the thirties reached the United States though several Yiddish silents were released with added sound tracks. Jewish characters did appear in films. Lev Kuleshov's *Horizon, the Wandering Jew* had Nikolai Batalov as the young Jew, Horizon, personifying the rise of the Jews to full citizenship under the Communist regime. Roshal's *The Oppenheim Family*, 1939, was anti-Nazi.

*The Return of Nathan Becker*, 1932 (United States release, 1933), was a classic propaganda film. Its obvious intention was to inform all Jews of the superiority of the Soviet system. Though it was made in both Russian and Yiddish versions by Belgoskino, only the Yiddish version was shown in the United States. Shlomo Mikhoels and David Gutman star. The film shows bricklayer Nathan Becker returning to his native Russia after twenty-eight years in the United States. Planning to share his expert knowledge with his fellow workers, he is disappointed to find them not receptive and prone to belittling his ability. He also finds that the people of his home town are different, infused with a "new spirit." He is beaten in a contest with other bricklayers and is about to give up and leave Russia when he is called by the chief of operations. Becker is then told that he may learn from the Russian workers and they from him. He sees the error of his ways and all is well.[26] *Nathan Becker* played at foreign film "art" houses, not at special screening geared to Jewish audiences.

*Seekers of Happiness (Birobidjan)*, directed by Vladimir Korsh-Sablin, 1934, was orginally shown in the United States as a short documentary. It follows another semidocumentary on the "Autonomous Jewish Republic of Birobidjan," Abram Room's *The Jew on the Land* of 1927. "A great documentary feature of the Autonomous Jewish Province in the Soviet

Union . . . [a] stirring epic of rehabilitation of old race in new land, stage by stage transformation of wilderness into fertile land. . . Soviet's reply to question millions of Jews throughout the world asking."[27] Later it was renamed *A Greater Promise* and released as fiction. A flyer includes photographs of each of the stars and claims that the film was "made under [the] supervision of S. M. Mikhoels . . . [and] includes Moscow Art Theatre Cast." It emphasized the theme of Jewish and Russian friendship. The story is about a group of industrious and cheerful Jews from abroad who settle on a collective farm in Birobidjan. They are contrasted with a Menachem Mendel type and the viewer is left to draw the conclusion that true happiness and worth come from the collective system. The film enjoyed a moderate success in America.

Worldkino also released a short of Yosel Cutler and his puppets. There were four scenes, *Simonas and His Wife*, *Kosher Dance*, *Peppery Jews*, and *Jazz*. This often played with new sound versions of *The Matchmaker* and *Laughter through Tears*. Joseph Burstyn reedited the latter, and Michael Rosenberg supplied a voice-over narration throughout the entire film.

The year 1934 marked the end of the early period of Yiddish film production. Jospeh Seiden directed no films in 1935, and Sidney Goldin, in his fifties, died that year. Sound films made the transition from disc to sound-on-film techniques, and it became easier to make films once again. Joseph Seiden, the self-styled "father of Yiddish films" who borrowed his idea from Sidney Goldin and two small films made in 1929, *East Side Sadie* and *The Eternal Prayer*, after an enthusiastic start in 1930, with three features and nineteen shorts began to have difficulty distributing his film. Those few producers who noticed Seiden's films were also unable to produce on a regular basis. One solution to filling the small market was to recut silent biblical films and add modern frame stories in Yiddish. This resulted in a quick and easy epic.

Nor could the small output of films from Europe make a continuous flow of production. It was not until Seiden sur-

## 1929–1934: THE YIDDISH TALKIE

faced in 1936 that Yiddish films reached their prime and others, who, like Maurice Schwartz and Joseph Green had attempted films in the early thirties, were able to produce on a continuous basis. Yiddish film was to boom from 1936 to 1941 with both Poland and the United States feeding a hungry audience. But, of course, it was already too late.

# 5 The Yiddish Cinema in America

While Joseph Seiden was the single most prolific producer of Yiddish films in the mid to late thirties, nearly half of the American films were made by independent producers who tried their hand at the market and then left discovering that a continuous supply of low-overhead films was necessary to make a buck. The situation in Poland was similar, although the Polish producers were never as prolific as their American counterparts. Polish films were made by Joseph Green, by a loose collective, and by independent producers. Unlike the American Yiddish films, which were completely out of the mainstream of the film industry, the Polish films often used native technicians and studios.

Joseph Seiden had his own studio, of a sort. After the two-year hiatus during which he changed his Judea Films to Jewish Talking Pictures (and soon after to Cinema Service Corporation), he was once again his flamboyant self. In 1936 he told the *Brooklyn Daily Eagle* all about his film productions. The reporter came to his studio at 33 West Sixtieth Street, Manhattan, grandly called Seiden Studios of the Talking Picture. (By 1939, Seiden had moved to Fort Lee, New Jersey.) It consisted of three rooms, a small sound stage, a laboratory which also housed the equipment, and a combination office and dressing room. The telephone was locked at all times. Seiden was just finishing *Love and Sacrifice*, "a gigantic super-production," shot in two weeks on a budget of $3,000 (this is a doubtful figure, for, in a later press release, Seiden claims costs of between $9,000 and $15,000 for his sound on film pictures). "It' [s a] bit more than the average picture. . . . We can turn them out in a week, if necessary."[1] How Seiden put together this film is typical of all his later productions.

Passover, the prime season for Yiddish films, was approaching, and Seiden had no idea for a story. In a bookstore on Allen Street he found a booklet, printed in Poland, called *Love and Passion* by Isadore Zolatarefsky. He bought the booklet for twenty cents, spent Saturday and Sunday rewriting it, and cast the film on Monday. "I get my casts very easily. I hang around the beaneries on 2cd Ave., there's always an actor who wants to get into the movies. I don't pay him nothing. Over a cup of coffee, I give him a smile and a promise and he's willing."[2]

The major props for the sets were made up of furniture from Seiden's home. Mob scenes were shot Saturday afternoons and Sunday, when all Seiden's friends would be available. There was, however, one minor problem about halfway through the film: the leading lady, Rose Greenfield, sprained her ankle and had to remain seated. But Seiden simply rewrote the scenario so all her parts would be close-ups and shot them in her own home.

Even though still in the cutting room, *Love and Sacrifice* was already being advertised at the Clinton Theater. When it was completed, Seiden would go to Chicago, sell the film there, and make arrangements for sending it further west. The film would play in every Jewish community in the United States of which Seiden was aware (accounting for his skipping most of the Midwest). World distribution would follow: France, Britain, Germany, South Africa, South America, and Canada.

The pictures used minimal union crews. There would be six or seven people: a cameraman, usually also the operator; an assistant; a soundman; an assistant soundman; and one or two

A South American poster for Maurice Schwartz's production of *Tevya*. Distribution networks were never very strong, but *Tevya* played all over the world. (Rutenberg & Everett Yiddish Film Library of the American Jewish Historical Society)

grips to push the dolly. There would also be a couple of electricians and two prompters. Sometimes Seiden himself directed and at other times he hired George Roland. His wife was the script girl, and a brother-in-law in the costume business provided the costumes. His son, Harold, was cameraman on the last few productions and also acted as film technician. Seiden could not read Yiddish, though he spoke it well enough, so someone had to write it in Latin script, i.e., Yiddish in English letters.

The camera was a standard Mitchell with a Fieldes dolly. Lights were at least deuces, the film needing 250–300 footcandles for exposure. It was all flat lighting, no fresnel lenses. Often the studio would get so hot that the crew worked in undershirts. Blocks of ice were kept on hand, and the workers would drape towels on the ice and wear the cloths around their necks. Shooting would stop from time to time so the actors could be "iced."

Movielab, Mercury Film Labs, and Criterion processed the films, but all special effects were done by Seiden. They shot the titles themselves and even did the fades by hand.

> I used to do my own fades. I used to take potassium ferrocyanide. We used to take the negative and I dipped it and held it in the potassium ferrocyanide, which is a bleach and every ten or fifteen seconds, I drop another frame. I put a two-foot fade on it, then I'd wash it out and we'd have our fade. A fade out and a fade in. We'd do it by hand because opticals were five, ten dollars a piece. You had thirty, forty opticals, that's $400. I would spend a couple of days and do it by hand.[3]

The Clinton Theater on the Lower East Side always had the first run for the Jewish Holidays. The films would literally be completed the day before. On Fridays, when the payroll had to be met, Seiden would go over to the theater and they would advance the money from the theater receipts.

Leo Fuchs, a leading comic actor in the Yiddish theater, starred in the 1937 *I Want to Be a Mother*. As Fuchs recalls, he was at the Cafe Royal and Seiden came over and asked, "Hey, how would you like to do this [picture]?" He was told the story and asked if he would star in it. Knowing nothing about film, Fuchs forgot to ask to see the script. "I was so excited about having my name above the title." He signed to do the film while he was appearing in a show and was supposed to shoot at midnight after the performance. Instead, Fuchs went home and went to sleep. Joseph Seiden came over and pulled him out of bed to do the shot. "We went up there, spoke our lines and set the camera and that's how we did it. I just did what they told me to do. Perhaps, when they were discussing the songs, maybe I made a *mensch* out of myself."[4]

Until 1941, Seiden continued with a steady output of films. Seiden himself never really knew how many films he made. Films might be copyrighted two or three years after they were made or not at all. Knowing that he could not really make a living at this, Seiden would often pick up films from laboratory auctions, thus providing himself with a larger library. A feature would be recut and sold as a different film. *I Want to Be a Boarder* was made from the outtakes of *I Want to Be a Mother*. This was indeed a rarity. With Seiden's low overhead, there would rarely be outtakes. *Mazel Tov Yidden* is a compilation of musical numbers from the shorts and features. "They took out songs I did and put them in other Jewish pictures and they starred me in those other Jewish pictures and all I did was one song," says Leo Fuchs.[5]

While Seiden joked about his "tearjerkers," calling the dialogue "sentimental and maudlin," he acknowledged that those were the films that made money. He sincerely believed that the "old fashioned entertaining, melodrama with music, comedy, song and dance has [had] the better chance of practical survival." While he personally would rather have produced a better grade of films, he felt this could only be done if such films were subsidized by a nonprofit group. He would point to his experience with *The Voice of Israel* as an example.[6] His son, Harold Seiden, said, "the Yiddish pictures were an ego trip, I think, for him."[7]

Seiden's films quickly settled into a formula that was copied by most of the Yiddish film producers. They were contemporary melodramas with convoluted plots, singing, religion, and the requisite happy ending. They concentrated on family conflicts, economic problems, and parent-child relationships, with an occasional lighthearted study of male-female loyalty. Money was usually the motivating force behind actions that led to separated families, adopted babies, and unloving marriages. These problems were always miraculously overcome by the end, usually through coincidence.

The situations demanded some sacrifice that the protagonist would be called upon to make—give up her baby, go to prison to protect the family, or leave all loved ones. These scenes always brought the audience to tears. In order to balance the sobs, comic interludes were always provided by minor characters such as quarreling neighbors, the village matchmaker, servants, an unexpected visitor, or the grandparents.

Other minor themes were found in most of the films. There was a great respect for learning, the learned person being portrayed with great dignity. Children were always cherished and the entire family revolved around them. Musical interludes were usual and most of the films contained singing and some dancing. Seiden employed some of the most popular Yiddish musicians, singers, and songwriters for his films. Cantor Leibele Waldman appeared in six features and a number of shorts. Sholem Secunda scored *Eli, Eli, Her Second Mother, The Jewish Melody,* and *Motel the Operator.* Sometimes the music was incorporated into the plot, though the films were rarely so sophisticated. Religious ceremonies were a common inclusion and were treated as part of everyday life. They included everything from the lighting of the Sabbath candles to the memorial service for the dead.

The top Yiddish theater actors starred in these films. Lazar Freed and Rose Greenfied appeared in *Love and Sacrifice.* Leo Fuchs, Hannah Hollander, and Yetta Zwerling topped *I Want to Be a Mother.* Ludwig Satz starred in *What a Mother-in-Law,* Lazar Freed in *The Great Advisor* and *Eli, Eli,* and Isidor Cashier in *The Jewish Melody.* It began to look like a stock company with Lazar Freed, Yetta Zwerling, Jacob Zanger, and Seymour Reichtzeit appearing in almost every film.

Comic interludes were a necessity. A scene from *The Jewish Melody*, 1941. (Rutenberg & Everett Yiddish Film Library of the American Jewish Historical Society)

Sheet music of the songs was released with such titles as " 'America' by Max Schwartz sung by Harry Feld in Joseph Seiden's motion picture triumph 'Mein Sindele' (My Son)."

The plot of *Her Second Mother*, starring Esta Salzman and Muni Serebroff, is complicated.

> Jonah Steinfeld, a young lawyer, is touring with his wife Florence, when they are caught in a terrible storm on a mountain road. Florence is expecting a baby in a few months. He finds a doctor in the farmhouse of Moishe and Esther Polokoff, attending their daughter Bella. Jonah sets out to bring the [doctor's] instruments and never returns. His young wife dies in childbirth.

The baby Sarah lives and Mr. and Mrs. Polokoff bring her up. Eighteen years pass. Sarah believes that the Polokoffs are her parents. Sarah, now a private secretary, learns that her sister Bella is carrying on an affair . . . with the bookeeper in her office. [The bookeeper] hides money that he stole from his employer's safe with Bella. About to be found out, he involves Sarah who takes the blame in gratitude to her foster parents. The truth is discovered and the story ends on a happy note. The District Attorney, Nathan, marries Sarah and we see both grandparents, Jonah [the judge who tried the case and turns out to be the missing father] and Moishe, delighting in the joys of their new grandson.[8]

*I Want to Be a Mother*, released in 1937, is another case of mistaken identity. Celia, the illegitimate daughter of Amelia, is raised by her brother and his wife as their daughter. Celia marries a young physician and lest Amelia reveal her secret does not attend the ceremony. Neither does the bridegroom's father. Six months pass and Celia suspects Amelia of being in love with her husband. Amelia agrees to leave until Celia's jealousy passes but breaks down and hysterically proclaims that she is Celia's mother. The two embrace. The young husband's father arrives and Amelia recognizes him as the man who disgraced her twenty years ago. Celia has married her own brother! All ends happily as the father reveals that his son is adopted and then marries Amelia.[9]

The realism and horrors of sweatshop life are portrayed in *Motel the Operator*, 1940, based on the Sholom Aleichem stories. In 1920, Motel is injured when he strikes for better wages. Motel is hospitalized for ten years, having "lost his reason," and his wife places their son up for adoption. Motel returns to his old neighborhood, where he is no longer remembered and must scrape to get by. Meanwhile, the man who arranged for the son's adoption has been blackmailing the foster parents. Years pass and the son becomes a lawyer. Mr. Benson hires the starving Motel to help him with his deceit, but upon meeting the family Motel realizes what a wonderful upbringing his son has had and foils the plan. A fight takes place and Motel accidentally shoots Mr. Benson and is arrested. His son, who knows nothing of Motel, de-

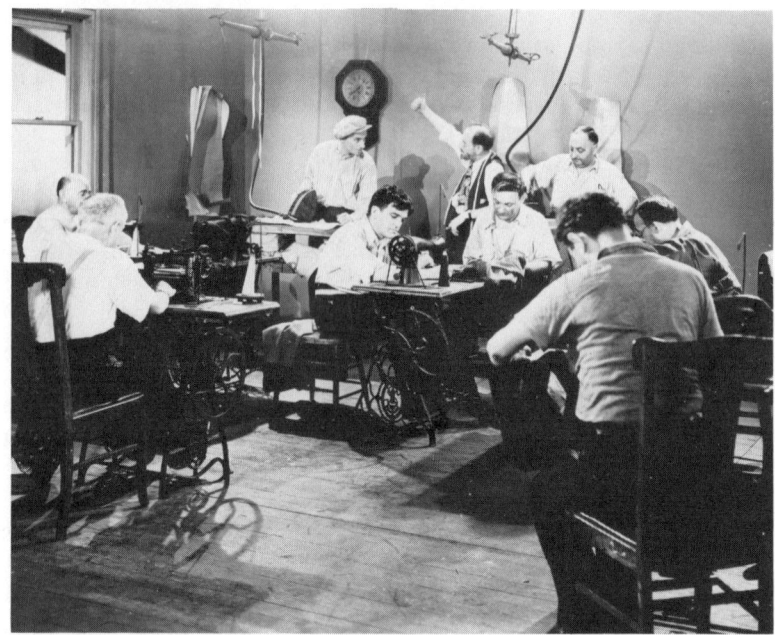

The reality of contemporary Jewish life: the New York sweatshop. Chaim Tauber in Joseph Seiden's production of Sholom Aleichem's *Motel the Operator*, 1940. (Rutenberg & Everett Yiddish Film Library of the American Jewish Historical Society)

fends him successfully. Motel is invited to live with the family. He attends his son's wedding where an old shopmate recognizes him. Motel begs him to keep the secret and the film closes on the happy wedding scene as performed by Cantor Leibele Waldman.[10]

*The Great Advisor* encompasses another favorite setting: the entertainment world. In this, a radio advice-giver attempts to advise his listeners but is unable to help himself. He meets a marraige broker and a third schemer. One of the letters sent to the advisor is from a rich widow looking for a husband. The advisor decides to marry her himself and the marriage broker sets up the match. However, the advisor's sweetheart catches him with the widow and instigates a hair-pulling match, which has the poor advisor getting the worst of it. The lottery ticket salesman sells tickets on the outcome of the match. The plot continues and ends with the advisor marrying the widow and the marriage broker marrying the former sweetheart.[11]

While the plots of Edgar G. Ulmer's films at times sounded like Joseph Seiden's, his approach and treatment were the antithesis. Best known for *The Black Cat*, 1934, and now a popular cult figure, Ulmer also directed films in Yiddish and Ukrainian, earning him the title "Director of Minorities."[12] Ulmer faced the same financial conditions as Seiden but had had years of practice in overcoming such limitations, had a sincere desire to create artistic works, and entered the field of Yiddish films when there was already a proven audience.

Ulmer had no Jewish upbringing and did not even know that he was Jewish until he reached high school. Running away from home, he met Rudolph Schildkraut, and during his first visit to New York, Schildkraut introduced him to Maurice Schwartz's Jewish Art Theater. Ulmer was enthusiastic about the productions, especially Peretz Hirschbein's *Greene Felder (Green Fields)*. On one visit, he said, "[I] met a group of youngsters, one of whom had bought [brought] a film made with Molly Picon in Warsaw. That film made a fortune in New York. Unbelievable."[13]

Ulmer entertained the idea of making a film of *Green Fields,* and when he was called to New York in 1937 to make a Ukrainian picture this seemed the right time. He managed, with great difficulty, to obtain permission from Hirschbein to use the play. There was one condition: Jacob Ben-Ami, who had played the leading role of the young Talmudic scholar fifteen years previously, must star once again. Ulmer agreed, though neither he nor Ben-Ami wanted this.

In seeking funds for the production, the three major New York Yiddish papers, the *Forward, Der Tog* ("the day"), and *Freiheit* ("freedom"), each wanted to back the film. Ulmer refused. "It was impossible—I couldn't take the readership of any paper with me because I would ruin the box office." There was one solution, "Everyone of us, the producers, hocked the furniture in his home," and they borrowed $8,000 from Household Finance.[14]

"Now I declared war the first moment I went into [the] picture—I'm not going to do what Schwartz does, I'm not going to do the cheap things which Picon does, I'm going to have my own style and I'm going to do it like I see it—dignified, not dirty—not with beards where they look like madmen."[15]

Roman Rebush acted as executive producer for Collective Film Producers, Inc. They shot in Flemington, New Jersey, on the same farm and with the same sets which he had used for his nationalistic Ukrainian film. The specially built thatched roofed houses were a perfect re-creation of Hirschbein's isolated rural village. "There was no electricity, no telephone poles, nothing."[16] Ben-Ami was given the title of codirector, which fulfilled the obligation to Hirschbein, and he acted as a gobetween for actors and director, for Ulmer knew no Yiddish. The lead went instead to Michael Goldstein (later Gorin) of Artef.

They rehearsed for six weeks and shot the film in five days. "The assistant and I had to sleep in the same bed in a brokendown hotel in Newark. I mean, we were so poor, you have no idea. We had nothing but ambitions." Collective Film Producers could only afford 15,000 feet of negative for the two-hour film so Ulmer shot 1¼ to 1. He had one lucky break, the first BNC (blimped news camera) and "lots of cooperation."[17]

This charming, pastoral film was a new experience for the actors. The Yiddish theater was known for its histrionics, but Ulmer wanted a more realistic style and none of the melodrama associated with the former. For the young Herschel Bernardi, who had grown up in the tradition of the *shund* theater, this was his first art production.

With shooting completed, Ulmer made a deal with the laboratory. They gave him ninety days credit on a $3,000 bill. If Ulmer could not pay the lab what he owed by the end of this period, the lab took the negative. During this time, Ulmer had to cut the picture, rerecord the sound, and find

Herschel Bernardi and Michael Goldstein in Edgar G. Ulmer's *Green Fields*, 1937. This was Ulmer's first Yiddish film and Bernardi's first "art" production. (Rutenberg & Everett Yiddish Film Library of the American Jewish Historical Society)

music for it. On the ninetieth day he was cutting negative. Illya Lopert, owner of the sound studio and the laboratory, informed him that if he did not have the $3,000 by eight o'clock the next morning, they would foreclose on the film.

In desperation he approached Abe Cahan of the *Forward*. Cahan, in turn, contacted David Dubinsky of the International Ladies Garment Workers Union and Ulmer told him his story. Dubinsky replied, "What are you so excited about? Can I see the picture tonight?" The film was still in rough cut. "If it's a good picture we will buy 75,000 tickets for the New York run. . . . I will give you $20,000—$5,000 tomorrow if I like the film. . . . I am paying you for a ticket 40¢. I can sell it for whatever I want to my Union members—you have no box office Monday, Tuesday, Wednesday, Thursday, Friday."[18]

The union representatives loved the film. The following morning, at 7:30, Ulmer got his money to pay the laboratory. He also made a new agreement to split the house on Friday nights, half for the union and half "because we have a negative to pay off."[19] Ulmer paid the laboratory, moved the print to another laboratory across the street, and had $2,000 remaining for publicity, a theater, hiring an orchestra, and otherwise finishing the film. With the help of Fidelson Meyer, a lawyer, Ulmer hired a twenty-four piece orchestra, and as there was no cash, he paid them with a box-office warrant. The musicians could go to the box office and would be paid out of the receipts.

Jean Pica, the chief booker for the Loew's circuit, asked to see the film. Having been successful the previous year with Joseph Green's *Yiddle with His Fiddle*, he offered them $25,000 outright. Figuring he had a hit, Ulmer refused. On the way home to the Bronx, Ulmer passed the Squire Theater, where workers were busy putting up a new marquee. He got the name of the theater owner and walked over to his apartment. Even though he was planning to open the theater with *Mayerling*, Ulmer convinced him to take *Green Fields* by offering 20 percent of everything except the union tickets. They signed for a ten-week run.

*Green Fields* was a success. This quiet, pastoral comedy-drama about a scholar fleeing the city life received rave reviews from all the critics except Frank Nugent of the *New York Times*. (Soon after the review appeared, Nugent lost his position.) The audience loved the film so much that they refused to leave the theater after the performance, wishing to remain for a second showing. The manager had to stop the performance and call in the police. Still with no money to spend, Ulmer was given open accounts for advertising by the *New York Times* and the *Herald Tribune*. After twenty weeks downtown, *Green Fields* played the Loew's chain on a percentage basis. The film eventually made $50,000 in New York at a time when top theaters charged 55¢ per ticket. All this on a $16,000 negative!

Flushed with the success of *Green Fields,* Ulmer again directed for Collective Film Producers. This time he chose a version of David Pinski's *Yankel der Schmidt* retitled *The Singing Blacksmith.* Because of the success of *Green Fields,* Ulmer had complete control over *Blacksmith.*

Once again Ulmer faced the problem of making a film on a limited budget. With his usual resourcefulness, he combined *Blacksmith* with another Ukrainian production and set out to "build a home for the *Blacksmith,* a *stettel* [*shtetl*] or little Jewish village, a ghetto town."[20] Next to it, he was going to build his Ukrainian village. With shooting set to begin in June 1938, Ulmer and his staff set out in May to comb New York State.

No one was interested and he decided to return to New Jersey. Unable to afford a generator, they contacted City Service and followed the electric high line. The first week in June, while following an old dirt road, they found the perfect piece of land: a lake, sloping ground, no electric lines in sight. It was a Catholic monastery. The monks were enthusiastic about the picture, telling him, "the Catholic Church has always sponsored the arts."[21] They even volunteered to play the parts of the townspeople, as all the brothers had beards. Later, Ulmer found that on one side of the monastery was Camp Siegfried, the Bundist camp, and on the other, a nudist camp. At night, the monks stood guard so nothing would happen to the sets. When the film opened in October in New York City, the "entire Catholic clergy of New Jersey arrived in full regalia to see the picture."[22]

*The Singing Blacksmith* received good reviews that complimented the acting, setting, and facilities. *Variety* compared Moishe Oysher to all the previous stage Yankels and said, "Surely there has been no voice that has equaled the booming powerful baritone of Oysher as the singing blacksmith."[23] Oddly, no one mentioned one peculiarity. Herschel Bernardi, in one of his last roles before a temporary retirement, played the part of Moishe Oysher as a boy. By the time his scenes were completed, he was taller than Oysher the man.

Collective Film Producers planned four more films for the 1939–40 season—*Uriel Acosta, Riverside Drive, Yankee Boile,* and *Idle Inn*—but they were never made.

Ulmer found other funding for his Yiddish films. Under the name Carmel Productions, he produced and directed *The Light Ahead* with Isidor Cashier, Helen Beverly, David Opatoshu, and Yudel Dubinsky.

Chaver Paver wrote the screenplay based on Mendele Mocher Seforim's *Fishke der Krumer (Fishke the Lame)* and *Di Klatshe.* David Opatoshu played the part of Mendele, the bookseller who wandered from village to village selling books with a horse and wagon. They needed a young actor who spoke Yiddish fluently, "And there weren't too many around, very young ones, that is."[24] He received the magnificent sum of $500 for the part.

Ulmer used the same location as *Green Fields* for the field and river scenes. By this time he was not looking for a new location for each film. Interiors were shot in an old warehouse in New Jersey where they also built miniature sets for some of the exteriors. As Ulmer still knew very little Yiddish, Cashier also acted as dialogue coach.

The atmosphere was relaxed and friendly. Cashier had been in several films and Helen Beverly was already the "Queen of the Yiddish Cinema," complete with stage mother. It was Opatoshu's first film, and gradually he learned not to perform for the second balcony. For the first camera take, Cashier told him where to stand in their scene. Ulmer said, "Action," and Cashier took a step back, which meant that Opatoshu had to turn slightly in order to talk to him. "Which photographed my right ear." So Opatoshu took a step back. Cashier said no, he was supposed to stay where the mark is. "Cut! We start again. Line up. Action. He took a step back. I took a step back. This went on. I had to pay most of the time. I caught on very quickly [to] being knifed."[25]

*The Light Ahead* did not do well. Herschel Bernardi, who played a minor role, did not even remember the film's being released. A romance between a blind girl and a lame boy, complicated by a cholera epidemic and the smug attitude of the town fathers toward a hospital and medical project, it probably hit too close to the immigrant's recent memories. For his final Yiddish film, in contrast, Ulmer chose one that would laugh its way into its audience's heart, *Americaner Shadchen (The American Matchmaker)*.

Produced by Mr. Rubenstein of *Der Tog, Americaner Shadchen* featured Leo Fuchs in the title role. Judith Abarbonal played the young Jewish girl whose mother tried to marry her off through Fuchs's marriage bureau. After the usual numerous complications, the happy ending had Fuchs marrying her. Filmed on the same interior sets as *Green Fields,* Fuchs said that Ulmer had some approach, but still did not know Yiddish.

Calling cards advertised the film, "Interested in Matrimony? We Get Em—You Wed Em—See the *Americaner Shadchen.*"[26] It was Ulmer's last Yiddish film. The year was 1940.

Ulmer's films were unlike any of the other Yiddish films. He brought to them the experience of years of low-budget filmmaking and the sincere desire to make as good a film as possible within the restrictions of budget and form. Whether he saw any of Seiden's films is questionable, but he did have Joseph Green's and at least one of Maurice Schwartz's directorial efforts to use as a means of negative comparison.

Ulmer's films did not follow the traditions of either the Yiddish stage or the Yiddish cinema. *Green Fields* is a gentle comedy, not at all in the melodramatic tradition. A young Talmud student arrives at a Jewish farm in czarist Russia. The David-Noich family leads a simple, uncomplicated life and they employ the student to teach their son the *alef-beth*. His knowledge is treated with great respect. The only subplot concerns a neighboring farmer who wishes his daughter to marry the scholar. The daughter in turn is in love with David-Noich's son. Plans to educate the son are not successful, for it is the daughter who shows the aptitude for learning, covertly spying on her brother's lessons. After much bickering and

Moishe Oysher as the romantic Yankel and Florence Weiss as Rivke, the other woman, in Edgar G. Ulmer's production of *The Singing Blacksmith*, 1938. The handwritten "Overture to Glory" shows the care Joseph Seiden took with his collection of stills. (Rutenberg & Everett Yiddish Film Library of the American Jewish Historical Society)

arguing, with the neighboring farmer's family playing the part of the comic relief, the scholar decides to remain on the farm and marry David-Noich's daughter.

The film appeals to the supposed simplicity of the immigrants' past life. It lacks the plot complications of Seiden's contemporary melodramas and spends less footage on coincidence to further the story than on the natural development of events. It is romantic without being frantic. Based on one of the classics of the Yiddish art theater, this film gave Ulmer a better starting point than Seiden. One does not have to shudder at the thought of what Seiden would have done with this material; he would never have considered it.

*The Singing Blacksmith,* on the other hand, is more of a romantic melodrama. It stars a given Jewish box-office draw, the handsome, and, as it turns out, credible actor Cantor Moishe Oysher. Again, the setting is the farming area of the Ukraine. Oysher is the town's popular and handsome young blacksmith, who had been apprenticed as a child and had absorbed the values of fine craftmanship from the previous smithy. On the smith's death, he inherited the business. The young man's theme in life is to eat, love, and be merry. He makes the rounds of the local women but becomes enamored of a young orphan from the city. They marry and have a child. When a former love leaves her husband, she seeks asylum with the smith, partially to teach her husband a lesson and also to seduce Oysher again. She never quite succeeds but causes unrest and jealousy in the household and scandal in the town. All is forgiven by the young wife the following day and they live happily ever after. Comic relief of a sort is provided by Anna Appel's matchmaker.

*The Light Ahead* emphasized the poverty and suffering of the past, specifically Poland in the 1880s, and worst of all, the superstition of the town elders. Two young lovers, the blind Hodel (Helen Beverly) and the lame Fishke (Isidore Cashier) quarrel when the girl refuses to marry and leave the village to go begging in the city. Opatoshu, as the kindly bookseller, tells them that the future is filled with hope. Some of the village girls go swimming on the Sabbath and a cholera epidemic breaks out, causing the villagers to blame this defilement of the Sabbath. According to tradition, the poorest girl and boy in the village must be wed in the cemetery in order to appease the evil spirits. The town council so decrees, and Fishke and Hodel wed and ride out of the town with the bookseller to start a new life.[27]

*The Americaner Shadchen,* though a comedy, is contemporary to any film made in 1940. Leo Fuchs plays a movie star unlucky in love. He is the victim of seven or eight broken engagements (as the film begins, his latest fiancée has decided to return to her old love.) On the advice of his friends he sets up a free marriage bureau and is remarkably successful in

Leo Fuchs is the *Americaner Shadchen* being picketed by his more traditional colleagues. Fuchs offers his services free as a means for finding a wife for himself in Edgar G. Ulmer's original comedy, 1940. (Rutenberg & Everett Yiddish Film Library of the American Jewish Historical Society)

making matches. So successful in fact that he is picketed by the other *shadchens*. His solution is to hire them as partners. Fuchs falls for a young girl, Judith Abarbonal, but in his self-sacrificing manner tries to make a "good" match for her with a dull businessman. All ends happily as he marries the girl and the bore is married to the appropriate girl.

This is a slick, romantic comedy. Fuchs is as handsome as any movie star, and frequent comments are made by his clients to this effect. He lives in a stylish apartment in a good section of New York City, though he sets up his bureau in the Bronx. He even has a proper English butler, who, when the guests leave, lapses into a pure Brooklyn accent and slang-laden Yiddish. One is given the impression of two worlds: the English-speaking one outside, where one acts in a given manner, and the closed world of Jews, albeit successful ones, wherein one speaks Yiddish and may relax. Comic asides are supplied by improbable matches, such as that of a talkative woman to a deaf man, and by the other matchmakers. All the characters are attractive. There is the traditional happy ending.

What is most striking in Ulmer's films is their total lack of religiousness. Yes, the characters are Jewish, and yes, there is the traditional respect for learning—witness the families in *Green Fields*—but the obligatory scenes of religious ceremony are lacking. In the *Singing Blacksmith*, the only identification of the characters as Jewish is that they speak Yiddish. For the families in *Green Fields*, their Jewishness is accepted. Though they are far from any synagogue or rabbi, they are aware of being Jews, and nothing will change this. In *Americaner Shadchen*, Ulmer makes use of the folk institution of the matchmaker and pokes fun at the good match, but again the only major identifying factor of Jewishness is the language. One must also remember that Ulmer was not raised in a traditional Jewish family; he even attended a Catholic university. He spoke good German but was still able to capture the common-usage Yiddish of everyday folk in *Americaner Shadchen.*

It was with *The Light Ahead* that Ulmer made a mistake.

The leads, although played by attractive actors, were cripples. The village elders were ridden with superstition and the memory of such an unappealing tradition as marrying a couple in a cemetery to rid the town of evil spirits must have struck an unpleasant memory in the audience. Though the immigrants were long gone from these isolated Eastern European towns, the memories were still fresh. Ulmer showed the elders as wrong, a blow to tradition. It is one thing to treat superstition with dignity as the Polish production of *The Dybbuk* did, but it is unforgiving to mock these horrors. *The Light Ahead* was not a success.

If it can be said that Joseph Seiden had a counterpart, it would be Henry Lynn. Henry Lynn himself remains a mystery, and little survives of his works. Over a period of six years, Lynn was associated with eight films as writer/director. His productions are similar to Seiden's, though at times they are of an even lower technical quality, and he also was based in New York. Producers vary from film to film. Apparently Lynn needed to seek out separate funding for each.

*The Youth of Russia* of 1934, for Sov-Am, was Lynn's first Yiddish production. It depicted the conflict between ancient religious customs and present-day ideas of life and marriage in Russia. Wolf Goldfadden starred as a former lumber dealer who becomes a shoemaker under the Soviet regime. Gertrude Bulman played his daughter, a scandle to him as she frequently changes marriage partners.

His second film, *Bar Mitzvah,* released in 1935, was a guaranteed blockbuster as it starred Boris Thomashevsky, the matinee idol of the Yiddish stage. The plot, typically complex, involves a mother lost at sea and the subsequent remarriage of the husband, played by Boris Thomashevsky. The family is torn between those that dislike the father's intended and think he should wait and those that wish the marriage to take place. The mother conveniently reappears on the day of her son's bar mitzvah and thwarts the evil intentions of the second wife. Tears flow freely as the family is reunited.

*Shir Hashirim (Song of Songs),* 1935, stars Samuel Goldenberg as a middle-aged composer struggling to resist a young woman who has also inspired his latest opera, *Shir Hashirim*. There is a faithful, forgiving wife, and comic relief is supplied by twin grandfathers.

Lynn's *The Power of Life* is about a bookkeeper who sacrifices everything for his motherless children only to have them desert him. All ends happily.

*Mothers of Today*, 1939, stars Esther Feld as a widow who fights to keep her two children loyal to custom. The son forsakes his career as a cantor to marry a modern woman, and the daughter elopes with a gangster. Mother love triumphs as the daughter returns home and the modern daughter-in-law becomes a good, pious, Jewish wife.

*Where Is My Child?*, 1937, based on *Forgotten Mothers* by Sam Steinberg and William Segal, is an example of a tearjerker that also presents a social problem. Celia Adler, in her best Second Avenue style, plays a young mother widowed on the boat trip to America. Lost in a strange land, she decides to put her infant son up for adoption. Minutes after giving up her child, she changes her mind and returns to claim him. The head of the orphanage refuses, saying that she has renounced all rights. Adler finds the parents and begins to pester them, demanding her child back. The head of the orphanage convinces them that she is insane, and she is committed. Twenty-five years pass. The son has grown up and become a doctor. He is planning his wedding. One of the patients, in his asylum, a very timid woman who keeps begging for her child, holds a special interest for him. Secretly she twists the sheets into a doll and, rocking her "child" in her arms, croons him to sleep. Meanwhile the son's adopted family are throwing a party to celebrate the son's engagement. He insists on inviting one of his patients, this poor woman. She is brought to the house and is recognized by the head of the orphanage as the woman who brought this child to him twenty-five years previously. He repents and tells the new parents and son. All is forgiven and mother and son are reunited. Adler goes to live with her son and his new wife.

The overwhelming critical reaction to Lynn's films was disapproval of their technical inadequacy. His plots, all melo-

Henry Lynn never learned to direct, but it did not hinder Celia Adler's acting in *Where Is My Child?*, 1937. In this publicity still she is crying over her loss of her son's childhood, as he was taken from her as an infant. The films often treated real but melodramatic situations. (Rutenberg & Everett Yiddish Film Library of the American Jewish Historical Society)

dramas, and the acting leaned toward the worst of the *shund* theater. Lynn never managed to master the art of directing, and *Bar Mitzvah* is quite possibly the worst Yiddish film made. There are two setting, both rooms of an apartment. The entrance to the apartment, supposedly from out-of-doors, quite clearly shows a connecting room. Only the medium shots are in focus. There are neither fades nor dissolves, only wipes, and no two shots match in tone or focus. Under the dialogue is the noise of the camera. Two years later, Mr. Lynn managed to keep the camera in focus by the simple act of never moving it. All the action takes place center stage, and when a character is through in a scene, he or she walks off.

But the most ingenious of Mr. Lynn's tricks, even more so than the recutting of silent film for sound, was his production of *A People Eternal* in 1939. Lynn acquired the rights to the 1935 British production *The Wandering Jew*, directed by Maurice Elvey. The film is considered anti-Semitic. It tells of the Jew who spat on Jesus as he was being carried to Calvary and of his being doomed to wander the earth until Jesus returns. Lynn cut the film from 111 to 65 minutes, removed the references to Jesus, and dubbed in the voices of Ben Adler, Zena Goldstein, Leon Schecter, Lillian Bloom, and Max Rosenblatt. *A People Eternal* became a series of loosely connected scenes of the Jew's survival in the Roman Empire and during the Spanish Inquisition. It was advertised appropriately as the "First Million Dollar Yiddish Spectacle with a cast of 10,000."[28]

A number of producer/directors tried their hand at the Yiddish market, but pulled out after just one film. Maurice Schwartz, seven years after *Uncle Moses*, made *Tevya*. Schwartz had originally wanted to make Sholom Aleichem's version of his work on tour in Poland in 1936, but Joseph Green disagreed, and the idea was dropped. It was not until 1939 that Schwartz realized his dream. Based on the play, the segment of *Tevya and His Seven Daughters* in the film is of the daughter, Chave (Miriam Riselle), who converts and marries a Ukrainian intellectual (to end up washing his family's clothes). Heartbreak piles upon disgrace, and she is married in the Russian Orthodox Cathedral, dressed as a Ukrainian peasant girl. Tevya goes into mourning: he has no daughter. Later the mother dies and the daughter is not allowed to comfort her aggrieved father. Only when the townspeople, both pitying and scared (after all, Tevya has tea with the priest), force him to leave does the family reunite for the traditional happy ending. Tradition is the keynote, for Tevya, only an ignorant milkman, follows the way of his ancestors and even attempts to quote from the scriptures. Custom once

Tevya (Maurice Schwartz), though exiled, refuses to sell his beloved horse to Mikita (David Makarenko). Based on Sholom Aleichem's own adaptation of his stories, *Tevya*, 1939, was directed by Maurice Schwartz. The film focuses exclusively on the story of Chava, who marries a Ukrainian intellectual. (Rutenberg & Everett Yiddish Film Library of the American Jewish Historical Society)

again wins out over the new way, for the daughter who marries a gentile repents later and returns to her father in his hour of most need.

Henry Ziskin produced and Schwatz directed and played the title role. It was shot in Jericho, Long Island, and, as the *New York Times* said, "nobody has ever seen a more typically Russian locale, even in Soviet pictures."[29] Though Schwartz had total control of the film, as of his theatrical work, "He knew very little about filmmaking, as such, they used to photograph the plays, that's all. Take a studio and photograph the plays."[30]

## THE YIDDISH CINEMA IN AMERICA 99

After his success with *Green Fields,* Roman Rebush joined with Ludwig Landy and Ira Greene in a combine. Rebush and Landy were partners, each having an interest in the other's films although neither would take part in the actual work of the films of the other. Rebush had his own production company, Credo Films, and Greene and Landy would work through Elite Productions, Inc. There would be a mutual distribution system. Only two films were completed under this agreement.

Rebush finished *Mirele Efros* (often called the *Jewish Queen Lear*) first. It stars Berta Gersten as Mirele, a wealthy and shrewd widow at odds with her daughter-in-law's goal to free her son from her mother's domination. The film has all the power and grandeur of Jacob Gordin's stage play, but Joseph Berne, the director, and Ossip Dymov, the screenwriter, were no Edgar G. Ulmers. The film is entirely stagebound.

Greene and Lande's production was the overly ambitious *Overture to Glory.* They hired Sam Rosen (formerly with Joseph Seiden) as associate producer and cameraman and Max Nosseck as director. Nosseck, born in Poland, had directed in Germany and Spain for Paramount and United Artists. This was his first work in the United States. Ossip Dymov wrote the script about a cantor who forsakes his synagogue for the Austrian opera. As played by Moishe Oysher, he leaves his loving wife and goes off to the bright lights of stardom. Guilt turns him to drink. Hearing of his son's death (at the height of his success), he loses his voice. Roaming from city to city, he returns by chance to Vilna on the Day of Atonement. His voice miraculously returns and he sings the "Kol Nidre" and dies. An unhappy ending was their first mistake, though the old ways win in the end. The film itself is beautiful to behold, on a par technically with any film of its time. Almost forty years later, Martin Nosseck, head projectionist, still bemoans the fact they they made the film in Yiddish, thereby limiting the audience.

Rebush made plans for a film starring Victor Chenkin, written by Joseph Berne and Lewis Jacobs. Greene and

Landy and crew moved to Hollywood and set up shop as the Hollywood Yiddish Film Corporation at 1356 Gordon Street, on poverty row. Neither group ever made another Yiddish film.

A similarly plotted and themed film was *The Cantor's Son*, 1935, also starring Moishe Oysher. Perhaps the producers of *Overture to Glory* had seen *The Cantor's Son*, for Oysher plays a youngster living in a rural *shtetl* in Eastern Europe who runs away with a traveling theater troupe. Eventually he follows the troupe to America and grows up there. Things go badly until he is befriended by an East Side cabaret singer and is given a chance to sing. Fame and fortune follow as he becomes a success on the radio and a guest singer in synagogues. A letter from his parents on their golden anniversary brings him back to his little village, where his now-grown childhood sweetheart greets him. He decides to marry her. His sponsor from New York, who also loves him, travels to Europe to find him and arrives on their wedding day. Tearfully she gives him up for his first love. Michael Rosenberg supplies the standard comic character as the manager. Illya Motyleff directed for Eron Pictures (Sidney Goldin was originally signed as director but died before the filming was completed). *The Cantor's Son* is copyrighted by Mecca Film Laboratories, Inc., probably in lieu of payment of the laboratory bill.

Ben K. Blake's single directorial effort in Yiddish films, *Two Sisters*, 1939, is a somber domestic drama. The original screenplay by Samuel H. Cohen has Jennie Goldstein as an elder sister raising her motherless younger sister, played by Sylvia Dell. Goldstein sacrifices all so her younger sister can become a nurse. Both sisters love Muni Serebroff, a young doctor. Ben K. Blake ran advertisements announcing "1st of New Series of Jewish Features, in preparation 6 outstanding shorts for Major Release and 1 American Feature."[31] No other films followed.

*The Yiddish King Lear*, 1935, by Jacob Gordin, was produced by Johnny Walker and Jack Rieger and directed by

Harry Thomashevsky. This film may have been shot in Poland and edited in the United States as the footage is very limited. It may just have been shot on a low budget. Once again there is the patriarchal figure—this time played by Maurice Krohner—a wealthy Jew who decides to spend his latter years in Palestine. He leaves his estate to his son-in-law to divide among his three daughters. The two eldest take all the money, cutting off the youngest daughter and the aged parents, who are then forced to return. They stay with the son-in-law who treats them worse than the servants (who play the comic role). Only the youngest daughter, who has studied to become a doctor, against her father's wishes, remains true to him. In the end, the evil daughters are repentant and the parents and youngest daughter receive their rightful places of honor.

The audiences loved these films. They expected the formulas laid down by Seiden and were uncomfortable with the experimentation of Edgar G. Ulmer's *The Light Ahead*. Critics, on the other hand, were amazingly inconsistent in their reception of the films. They were completely fooled by the early sound/silent films, and such a knowledgeable trade paper as *Film Daily* did not recognize *Joseph in the Land of Egypt* as an amalgamation of old silent footage and new recorded sequences.[32] The *New York Times* did not seem to realize that Sholom Aleichem's *Tevya* antedated *Abie's Irish Rose*, "As for Sholem [sic] Aleichem, the author, he has simply restated the *Abie's Irish Rose* theme in a semi-serious vein, with the difference that in this case the orthodox point of view is triumphant."[33] *Variety* tended to be more informed, giving the complete stage history of theatrical adaptations such as *Mirele Efros*.[34] Yet the same review said, "Since Yiddish filmmaking is still in its comparative infancy, one hasn't learned to accept those productions on the same plane with their American counterpart." This was 1939, the penultimate year of production.[35] Critics could never decide whether the films were in "Yiddish," "Jewish," or "Hebrew." Frequently, Jews were referred to as Hebrews, and trade papers varyingly placed the films under "Features" or "Foreign." *Film Daily* solved the problem by placing any film not in English under "Reviews of the Films; Foreign."

Critics were especially hard on Joseph Seiden. "Action drags, production and direction are extremely crude and the acting varies from one extreme to another." "The actors do the best they can with the material." "Should you miss Mr. Seiden's first American production in Yiddish you will have nothing to reproach yourself for, providing that in your film fare you demand a certain amount of artistry, experienced direction, and smooth performances. [*I Want to Be a Mother*] is not graced by these things, in fact it appears to be a 'quickie.'"[36] While it is doubtful that the audiences read these reviews, Seiden was lucky that very few of his films were reviewed at all. The same was true of Henry Lynn's productions.

It is even luckier that the Jewish communities outside New York City never saw these reviews. In these communities the appearance of a Yiddish film, any Yiddish film, was greeted with unbounded enthusiasm. Distribution of the films outside the New York–Philadelphia area was undependable. In the first part of the decade, films were often hand-carried from town to town as Joseph Green did for *Joseph in the Land of Egypt* in 1932. *Joseph* played in Portland, Oregon, for six days from 13 October 1933—it ran in New York City during May 1932. The only Yiddish film that was ever shown in Iowa was *The Sacrifice of Isaac*, in Des Moines, November 1932. Russian films from the first half decade usually played in the local foreign art theaters. Yiddish films played wherever they could be booked.

A common method of showing a Yiddish film was to run it in the local Yiddish theater. Littman's People's Theater in Detroit filled the gaps in their stage bookings with films. In January 1939, they ran *Two Sisters* for two weeks of Friday, Saturday, and Sunday performances. Later in the month, *Uncle Moses* and the Polish *Der Purimspieler* played. In June, it was *Mothers of Today*, followed by three performances by the Yiddishe Bande and then, *The Light Ahead* in September.

In cities with a large Jewish population, the films would play for a week or two at a theater in a Jewish neighborhood. Cleveland is a case in point. Almost all the Yiddish features made in the decade of the thirties were shown in Cleveland. Smaller communities had a more difficult time. In Kansas City, Kansas, the films were rarely shown in theaters and were used as fund raisers. *Yiddle with His Fiddle* was presented by the Junior Haddassah, *The Cantor's Son* by the Shaaris Israel D'Lubawitz Synagogue, *Tevya* by Congregation Beth Hamedrash Hogodol, *Uncle Moses* (in 1938) by the same congregation, and *The Dybbuk* by another. Late in December 1939, *The Kansas City Jewish Chronicle* announced, "Cinema Theatre to Be Opened at Jewish Center." The center would be opening a new section to present the "quality" Jewish motion pictures now being made. The first film was *The Singing Blacksmith* screened on 1 January, 1940. There was never a second film.[37]

American films were only part of the story of the Yiddish cinema. For the rest, one must go to the Poland of 1936.

# 6    The Yiddish Cinema in Poland

Among the many things with which the Polish government was unable to cope was the sound film. With the introduction of talking pictures, the Polish government placed a 42 percent tax on the cinema's profits. Then the theaters were forced to pay for electricity at the much higher nonindustrial rates. Along with the propensity of Polish film producers to pay minimal wages to their technicians, the Polish film industry foundered during the first half of the thirties. Finally, Sphinx Films found that it was able to assure its workers an adequate living and also produce films that not only were profitable in Poland but were of exportable quality. The Polish public, who wanted films in their own language, supported the filmmakers.

    Joseph Green returned to Poland at this time to produce four Yiddish features and may have encouraged the Polish Jewish population to make their own films. In 1936 Green had come back to Poland with the rights to Henry Lynn's less than classic *Bar Mitzvah*. It was as enthusiastically received as the earlier *Joseph in the Land of Egypt*. Though Green felt that this was not a particularly good film, the name of Boris Thomashevsky and the sentimental morality of the piece had obviously appealed to audiences. He decided that now he would form his own film company and make a good Yiddish film. He set up an office in New York in the Paramount building as Sphinx Films and made arrangements in Poland as Greenfilm. It was 1936. No Yiddish films had been made in Poland since the silent era and the business in New York was just starting to thrive.

Using his own money, Green planned to spend $40,000–$50,000 on his first production. For this he could get the best technical staff in Poland, a new studio, and new equipment. The same film would cost about $200,000 if made in the United States.

Maurice Schwartz was on tour in Warsaw, so Green thought it would be a good idea to make the film with him. The film would be about Hotsmach, a minor character from a Goldfadden play. Schwartz liked the idea, and Green began to write the scenario about Hotsmach and his seven daughters. Then Schwartz changed his mind and told Green that he wanted to make *Tevya*. Green thought that, although *Tevya* would make a good movie, this was not the time, nor was Poland the place. The story would be too touchy because of Tevya's daughter marrying a gentile, and the family sitting *shivah* ("mourning") over her. Schwartz would later make *Tevya* in America.

Luckily, Molly Picon was in Paris, and Green started to look for a vehicle for her. From another writer, he got a story about a bride being stolen by musicians on her wedding day because she does not want to marry an old man. There was no part in it for Molly Picon. He changed one of the musicians to a girl who, in order to travel with her father, would disguise herself as a boy. The part would be perfect for Picon. The unhappy bride would then become a subplot, and Picon the film's central character. The film would begin with two groups of musicians who arrive in a neighborhood, which each group claims as its territory. Both bands begin to play at once, and the noise is so deafening that the people close their windows. Finally the bands play together, and the townspeople open their windows and throw down money. Green brought this idea to Picon and her husband, Jacob Kalich, in Paris. They liked the story and promised to go to Warsaw to make the film.

Green did not even have a title for the film. He brought Picon's composer, Abe Ellstein, to Warsaw, and Itzik Manger was engaged for the lyrics. Green settled down to write the scenario. One night the title *Yiddle with His Fiddle* came into Green's mind, and he immediately cabled Molly Picon in Paris to tell her the news. She cabled back, "We emptied twelve bottles of champagne on that title."[1]

The technical side of the film was handled by the Polish director Jan-Nowina Przybilski. Green directed the actors. Interiors were filmed in the studios in Warsaw, but for the exteriors Green had found a little Polish town, Kazimierz. This was not a Jewish town, though it was named after the mythical king of Poland who gave asylum to the Jews. The exteriors were very old; only the interiors were allowed to be modernized. They spent about two weeks there, renting an entire hotel and filming from 6:00 A.M. to 6:00 P.M. every day.

At one point in the filming they needed sixty peasants for a scene, all to be dressed in their Sunday best. The assistant passed the word that a Warsaw film company would be filming at seven o'clock Sunday morning and they would pay 5 zlotys per soul. That morning, the company set up the camera at six. From the top of the hill the crew saw the townspeople arrive—with their horses, cows, and goats. To the company it seemed as if thousands of people and animals were heading toward the town. The assistant had failed to specify how many people he needed and had not taken into account that in Polish a "soul" could also mean a cow, a horse, a child—indeed every living thing is a soul. Green spread the word that they were having trouble with the camera, and filming was postponed for a week.

The wedding scene was retained in the film, a hall being rented for the occasion. Green ran the scene like a real wedding. A kosher caterer supplied the food and as it was eaten or spoiled, so more food was brought in. All the poor Jewish townspeople were hired as guests. Green filmed all day and at eight o'clock at night had still not finished. At that point, he decided to film throughout the night or else lose the atmosphere (or possibly have to rent the hall for another day). More food was brought in. Couches were set up for the actors to sleep, but Green stayed awake the entire night to supervise the filming.

At four in the morning they were shooting a scene where rhymes are made up about the bride and groom. For tradition's sake, they needed a violinist. The assistants ran around the town and found one, and the film continued. One woman approached Molly Picon asking, "What is this?" She explained it was a wedding. "So why didn't you tell me?" she replied. "I could have brought my daughter and married her off." Green found the situation amusing. Molly Picon thought it was "very pathetic" that Green had not explained to the extras that they were acting in a movie.[2] They finished at 7:00 A.M.—twenty-eight hours of continuous shooting.

The film was a great success. It played first in Poland, and by the time it was released in America Green had broken even. It was the first Yiddish feature to play the major theater chains—Loew's, York, and United Artists. Reviews were generally favorable, calling *Yiddle* "tuneful, amusing entertainment."[3] Though it was mentioned that the film was in Yiddish, none of the reviewers gave it the usual condescending "good for its type" review. It was greeted for what it was: a technically proficient, period musical comedy that just happened to be in Yiddish. It was shown in Vienna, London, Paris, Belgium, Holland, South Africa, and Australia. And in Palestine it played in Hebrew.

*Der Purimspieler (The Jester)* followed in 1937. Joseph Buloff was originally cast as the lead in this love story set against the background of a traveling circus. The part was written especially for Buloff. When everything was ready and plans were made to return to Poland, Buloff was engaged in a play. Rather than wait for him or cancel, Green, considering that too much work and money had already been invested in the project, decided to go on with the film.

In Poland, Green engaged Zygmund Turkow to play the part of the purimspieler. "But he was not right for the part. He was too tall. He wasn't Buloff physically and he wasn't funny enough."⁴ But he was a fine actor. This was the first mistake. Then Green hired Nicholas Brodsky, later to work at MGM, to compose the music. "He was very famous, but he was not a Jewish composer."⁵ This was Green's second mistake.

Green needed religious Jews for many of the scenes, so instead of filming in Warsaw, where he would have to hire extras and provide costumes, he decided to film in Cracow in order to use the resident Orthodox Jews as extras. The company moved in with their cameras, and the assistants lined up the eighty or so extras needed. In the morning they set up in the town square, which the police had roped off for the shoot. The people were all there and waited for two hours until the crew was ready. When the crew looked up from their equipment, all the people were gone except for one man, who said, "I'll tell you what, the *rebbe* found out about it and he said, 'A man is created in the image of God. You're not allowed to be photographed.'"⁶ The next day Green hired actors and dressed them for the part.

For the filming, he engaged an entire circus. The little town would join the circus. Realizing too late that his film was no longer "Jewish," Green wished that he had made the circus a Yiddish theatrical company, possibly the original Goldfadden Troupe. He knew the film was well made, but the audiences felt that something was missing. And Turkow had not been right for the part. The critics again praised the film, but *Der Purimspieler*, which had cost more to produce than *Yiddle*, never made a profit.

Green still had money and hopes. He prepared *A Brivele der Mamen (A Little Letter to Mama)*. He wrote the story and hired M. Osherwitz of the *Forward* to cowrite the screenplay. Lucy Gehrman was cast as the mother and Mischa Gehrman as the head of the Hebrew Immigrant Aid Society (HIAS) in Poland. The story starts shortly before World War I with Lucy Gehrman as the mother supporting her family. The husband is despondent because he cannot find work and runs off to America to seek his fortune and then send for his family. The husband only makes enough to send for the youngest son. The war claims the other son, and the daughter runs off with a dancing master. After the war, the mother learns that her husband has died and her youngest son has disappeared. She goes to America, and with the help of HIAS a sorrowful reunion takes place.

Green prepared to leave for Poland and made arrangements for the Gehrmans to follow. Once more he engaged Abe Ellstein to write the music. Then Jacob Kalich approached Green. "What's the matter with you, Joe? You made a picture with Molly and the picture was a great success. You keep on making pictures. You don't make another one with Molly?" "Yankel, I'll tell you," replied Green, "I'd like to, if I would have a story. I didn't come up with a story." "Why not Molly's big success, *Mamele?* Why don't you make *Mamele* with her?"[7] Green had always been against making plays, feeling that movies should be original, but he also realized that he should do a follow-up film with Molly Picon. He agreed.

Green took the play with him to Poland and changed the American setting to a Polish one. The Gehrmans waited for six weeks while Green made *Mamele* first in Lodz. Molly Picon had just turned forty and in *Mamele* she had to play a twelve-year-old girl. A good makeup man created the miracle, and the filming was uneventful. Molly Picon played the middle sister who promises on her mother's deathbed to take care of the family—two sisters, three brothers, and a shiftless father. She saves them all from varying fates worse than death and finally rebels against her ungrateful charges. All ends happily, as usual.

It took about three months for Green to shoot both films. When they were finished in December 1938, he shipped out the negatives. He was convinced that war was coming to Poland. Green left soon after, taking all his papers with him, figuring that he would not be back in 1939. He had already made plans for someone else to release *A Brivele der Mamen* in Poland. "I told my friends that if there is no war in September and October, I would say I am wrong."[8] The war broke out in September 1939.

*Mamele* opened in New York in January 1939, to well-deserved good reviews. *A Brivele der Mamen*, which Green held until September of that year, totally eclipsed it. "The last Yiddish movie made in Poland before the Nazi invasion put an end, at least temporarily, to such activities is one of the best to reach here from that country," said the *New York Times*.[9] The *Motion Picture Daily* claimed, "*A Brivele der Mamen* deserves to be ranked with the foremost foreign films exhibited here during recent years."[10] Abe Cahan of the *Forward* wrote, "I was sitting here at the theater watching *A Brivele der Mamen* with mixed feelings. One side, I thought of the sacrifices in Poland on account of the war and the second, *A Brivele der Mamen*, the situation of the Jewish people in that film which is similar to my feeling what's happening now."[11] With Green's excellent timing in releasing the film and the fine acting of the Gehrmans, Green says it was the biggest box-office-grossing Yiddish film of all time. The Academy of Motion Picture Arts and Sciences even screened the film as a possible Oscar nominee.

The Polish Jews may have been fearful of the possibility of anti-Semitic actions from their neighbors and were afraid of encouraging them. This may have been the reason that no Polish filmmakers made Yiddish films until after Joseph Green's *Yiddle with His Fiddle*. The example Green set while working in the Warsaw studios probably encouraged the making of the few Polish productions that followed.

Yitzak and Shaul Goskind owned a film laboratory, Sektor. (Under Polish law, all prints of films shown in Poland had to be made in Polish laboratories.) With Shimon Dzigan and Israel Schumacher, the satirists, they formed a *kinor* ("collective"), a film cooperative of Jewish actors and artists. Their first production was an original drama, *Al Chet (I Have Sinned)*, produced by the Warsaw Art Players. The plot is similar to those of the American films of this era. It is the story of a village maid, Esther (Rachel Holtzer), who loves a soldier and becomes pregnant by him. But he is killed on the battlefield, so the unwed mother abandons her baby daughter. Much later, the mother, now a wealthy woman, seeks her

Ida Kaminska in the Polish film of Jacob Gordins's *Without a Home*, 1939. (Rutenberg & Everett Yiddish Film Library of the American Jewish Historical Society)

Dzigan and Schumacher in the Polish comedy *Jolly Paupers*. (From the archives of the YIVO Institute for Jewish Research)

lost child in America. The girl, who has been adopted, is now in love with a violinist. There is a happy ending, and Dzigan and Schumacher play the comic-relief roles.[12]

Two other fiction films from this group are *Without a Home (Ahn a Heim)* and *Jolly Paupers (Freylikhe Kabtsonim)*. Both had Dzigan and Schumacher providing comic relief. The former, from the Jacob Gordin play, revolves around a Polish immigrant family's trials and tribulations in New York. It has an unhappy ending. *Jolly Paupers*, on the other hand, is a light comedy about a promoter who plants oil on an old farm and tricks the local tailor who then brings in investors from all over. Both starred the Warsaw Art Players.

The most unusual film to come from this group is a documentary, *Mir Kumen On (Children Must Laugh)*. Alexander Ford had filmed a documentary, *Chalutzim*, in Palestine in 1934. It is a record of the building of the Jewish homeland and probably the first talking film made there. Knowing of this, Sektor asked Ford to again direct a scripted film with nonprofessional actors. It was written by Wanda Wasilevska about the Vladimir Mendem Sanitarium for tubercular children. It included a scene showing the children welcoming a group of gentile children whose fathers were on strike. The inclusion of this caused the film to be banned by the Polish censors.

The most widely known and celebrated of all Polish Yiddish films is the 1937 production of S. Anski's (S. Z. Rapoport) *The Dybbuk*. Ludwig Pryes approached the writer A. S. Kacyzna to adapt the play to the screen. Made by Fencke Film and directed by Michael Waszynski, a Polish Jew who learned his craft under Henry Szaro, it stars actors from the Polish Yiddish stage. The eminent Jewish historian Dr. Meyer Balaban aided with the historical research. Americans Jacob Mestel and George Roland were brought in for "interpretation" and editing.

In the 122-minute film, they treated the folktale with great reverance and endless attention to detail. Two weeks were spent on location for the outdoor scenes of Elijah and the

Lili Liliana as Leah, the young girl possessed by the soul of the dead student in the exorcism scene from *The Dybbuk*, Poland, 1937. The emphasis was on realism. (Rutenberg & Everett Yiddish Film Library of the American Jewish Historical Society)

town. Five weeks were spent in the studio in Warsaw. The folktale is of two men who pledge their unborn children to marriage. The two men part ways and when their children are grown up, they are betrothed to others. The poor student buries himself in the Cabbalah and dies, invoking the devil. He becomes a wandering, restless soul and enters his promised one's body. She has become a *dybbuk* which must be exorcised. Waszynski creates the moments of premonition through off-center frame compositions and unusual lighting. The *dybbuk*'s ghostly form dissolves on an open highway, vanishes, and reappears at will. This was probably the most successful Yiddish film made—the type of classic material that no one could ignore, and with all the trappings of the art stage. It was even reviewed in *Time* and *Newsweek*.

A few more productions trickled from Poland. *Neighbors*, 1938, is an interesting attempt by Best Films to capture the Jewish audience. It was first shown in New York City in January 1938, as *Piętro Wyżej (The Apartment Above)*, starring Helen Grossowana. In December of that year it was released as *Neighbors*, a Yiddish comedy with Helen Gross and the Warsaw Art Theater Players. The Polish version is the original. *The Vow (Tkijes Khaf)* is again the story of a marriage pledge made before the children are born and the prophet Elijah's ultimate intercession to make the vow true. This time it starred Zygmund Turkow as the prophet Elijah and Dina Halpern as the young girl. Henry Szaro directed this updated version of his 1924 film.

The war in Europe had come as Joseph Green expected. In September 1939 Hitler's armies marched into Poland and closed the film studios in Warsaw. Green was safely in New York City making unsuccessful plans for more films. Those Jews who could, fled, like Dzigan and Schumacher, to Russia to resurface after the war. Most died in the ghettos and concentration camps.

Yiddish film production continued in America for another two years but without the European markets. In 1939, Hollywood started to worry about the closing European markets. Production curtailment began. The number of films released in the United States dropped considerably, especially the independents. From a high of 407 in 1938, independent production dropped to 175 in 1942.[13]

In a press release dated 1941, Joseph Seiden wrote, "Cinema Service Corp. has a program of six films scheduled for the season 1941–1942." The sentence is crossed off. *Her Second Mother* and *The Jewish Melody*, 1941, were his last prewar productions.

Yiddish films had reached their peak of production and art in the second half of the 1930s. The formula films of Joseph Seiden and Henry Lynn dominated the field, but there was enough money and sufficiently enthusiastic audience for a few less traditional pictures. For a brief time, Yiddish films were to venture into the world of the art theater. Edgar G. Ulmer, an experienced low-budget-film director, stamped his signature on four highly individualistic films, while Joseph Green, in Poland, tried his hand at the true Yiddish musical comedy. But there was not enough time. The brief period of stability between the wars drew to a close much too quickly for the European Jews.

# 7   Aftermath

The Second World War ended, and once again the Yiddish film producers geared up for production. This time they were to be sorely disappointed. Six million Jews had died in Europe. From a purely materialistic viewpoint, there was no European Jewish audience. In the United States, a 1945 survey by the Yiddish Scientific Insitute (YIVO) showed that of the Jews immigrating to the United States before 1924 (when immigration was effectively cut off), 16 percent of the second generation knew no Yiddish. Of the third generation, 68 percent did not know the language.

When the Joint Distribution Committee officials visited displaced persons camps in Europe, they took Joseph Seiden's films with them. Nothing, officials assured Seiden, proved more uplifting to the DPs' morale than a showing of these films depicting Jews leading normal, if somewhat chaotic, lives and speaking Yiddish. *Yiddle with His Fiddle* was another favorite.

In 1946, Shaul Goskind returned from the Soviet Union to become the film librarian for the newly formed Film Polski. With Joseph Goldberg he organized another *kinor*, in Lodz, the new center of Polish film production. From 1946 to 1950 they made two feature-length films and twelve shorts.

*Unzere Kinder (Our Children)*, made in Warsaw from 1946 to 1947, is a semidocumentary about the orphans of Lodz, starring Dzigan and Schumacher. In postwar Warsaw two Jewish actors, played by Dzigan and Schumacher, give a seriocomic performance about the Warsaw ghetto. In the audience are some orphans from an orphanage outside Warsaw who become restless and disrupt the performance. Afterward, they come to the actors' dressing room and apologize, identifying themselves as the children from the ghetto who had outwitted the Nazis and survived. For them the film had evoked memories that were too painful to bear. The actors accept their invitation to perform at the home. At the performance, they both entertain and are entertained by the children. The actors leave the orphanage much wiser. *Unzere Kinder* was banned by the Polish government.

Nathan Gross also directed *Mielebn Gerleben (We Live Again)* for them. Beyond this, the records lapse. In 1952, Goskind was officially reprimanded and fled to Israel. He would later be joined there by Dzigan and Schumacher. His name has disappeared from the Polish film history books along with the records of all the films he produced between 1937 and 1950. In 1957, the Polish State Film Studios released a documentary entitled *Jews in Poland*. It included footage of Ida Kaminska in a brief performance of the new state-supported Jewish Art Players. This film has also disappeared.

Two other films came from Europe in Yiddish. *We Live Again*, produced in France by M. Baheifer, O. Fessler, A. Hamza, I. Holdodenka, and H. Weinfeld, is a documentary on the homeless Jewish children in Europe. It played in New York in 1948 with a musical short, *Overture to Glory*, and Yiddish dialogue newsreels produced in Russia. Italy produced a feature, *The Earth Cries Out*, 1949, on the struggle for the liberation of Palestine. It was dubbed into several languages, including Yiddish. The producers realized that there was a Yiddish-speaking audience somewhere.

Joseph Green made plans for a film with Moishe Oysher. He worked on it for a time, but Oysher died and nothing came of it. Green went on to buy a chain of theaters in New York and then into the distribution of films under the name Globe Pictures. In the mid-fifties, Molly Picon traveled to

London to make an English sound track for *Yiddle with His Fiddle*. The result was *Castles in the Air*—*Yiddle* with a British accent. Even the music was rerecorded. In 1956 it played in New York.

Joseph Seiden, the first to begin continuous production of Yiddish talkies, was the last to stop. He refused to give up and almost until his death in 1970 tried to keep Cinema Service in active production. In 1948, though claiming that no more films could possibly be made, he planned to produce a series of shorts of Jewish interest for 16mm institutional exhibition. These films were never made. In 1950, he put together *Monticello Here We Come*, a compilation film of musical numbers from his shorts and features of the thirties. The same year, he tried an original production, Jacob Gordin's *God, Man and Devil*. Aaron Film Corporation produced and Seiden, using the name Joseph Zeiden, directed. It starred Michael Michalesko, Gustav Berger, Max Bozhyk, and Jacob Ben-Ami in what was essentially a filmed play. Eleven years later he released *Three Daughters* with Michael Rosenberg.

The same year, 1950, Pictorial Ventures put together a modern Catskill Mountains–type Yiddish American vaudeville show, *Catskill Honeymoon*. Directed by Joseph Berne, it is a series of sketches tied together by a loose plot. Jewish Film Distributors, Jacob Mesterland and George Roland, re-released the 1933 *A Vilna Legend*.

It was all over. Yiddish films became a relic of the past and entered the nontheatrical rental circuit. Joseph Green sold the 16mm rights for *Yiddle* and *A Brivele der Mamen* to Audio Brandon (MacMillan). The negatives for *Mamele* and *Der Purimspieler* caught fire and were destroyed.

During the 1960s, Seiden kept Cinema Service alive as a rental company. He was able to advertise "33 Yiddish Film Classics." The titles for rent included many of his films, such as *The Great Advisor, The Jewish Melody, Love and Sacrifice,* and *Motel the Operator*. There were also Polish films like *Neighbors, The Dybbuk,* and *Chalutzim*. *The Singing Blacksmith, Bar Mitzvah, The Vow,* and *Americaner Shadchen* also turned up in his catalog. Although he did not have the

"MAZEL TOV YIDDEN"

The glory that was Yiddish films: a compilation of comic scenes and musical numbers from his shorts and features, Joseph Seiden's *Mazel Tov Yidden* is another example of his enterprise in making a buck. (Rutenberg & Everett Yiddish Film Library of the American Jewish Historical Society)

rights to most of these films, no one bothered him. His main audiences were synagogue benefits, but occasionally the films would play, all at once, on Second Avenue or in Miami Beach.

The issue was no longer the demand for new productions but the pettiness of how many cents per foot would be charged for a new print. Overseas he would sell the rights for five years at a cost of $1,000 in American funds plus 5¢ per foot for 35mm or 4¢ per foot for 16mm. At the end of five years they were supposed to return the prints, but of course they never did. Seiden's son Harold continued the business but gradually cut back on overseas rentals. The prints were not maintained, and each year some films were lost. In 1975 he sold his 35mm prints to a collector. In 1976 Harold Seiden decided that the business was too much bother and sold all the remaining films and papers to the National Jewish Media service of the American Jewish Historical Society. They set up the Rutenberg and Everett Yiddish Film Library to preserve and distribute the films. The era of Yiddish films was officially over.

# Notes

## Chapter 2

1. For a list of films with "Jews," see Stuart Fox, *Jewish Films in the United States: A Comprehensive Survey and Descriptive Filmography* (Boston: G. K. Hall & Co., 1976).
2. Decreed by Nicholas I in 1883. This included the provinces of Grodno, Vilna, Volhynia, Podolia, Minsk, Ekaterinoslav, Bessarabia, Bialystok, Kiev (except for the city), Khernson, Taurida, Moghilev, Vitebsk, Chernigov, Poltava, Courland, Livonia (Latvia), and the Kingdom of Poland.
3. For an in-depth study of Russian and Soviet film, see Jay Leyda, *Kino: A History of the Russian and Soviet Film* (London: George Allen and Unwin, 1960).
4. Ibid., p. 405.
5. John H. Snodgrass, "Motion Pictures in Foreign Countries," *The Film Index*, 28 January 1911, p. 4.
6. In *Kino*, Jay Leyda also lists *The Violin*. I have not been able to see this film, but reviews do not indicate any Jewish subject matter.
7. Review of *Lai Chyeim* in *The New York Dramatic Mirror*, 3 May 1911, p. 30.
8. *Encyclopaedia Judaica*, 1971 ed., s.v. "Motion Pictures."
9. *The Moving Picture World*, 23 May 1914, p. 1146.
10. "Sidney M. Goldin—a Director Who Achieves," *The Universal Weekly*, 2 August 1913, p. 32.
11. Review of *The Sorrows of Israel*, *The Moving Picture World*, 14 June 1913, p. 1180.
12. "A Trip through the Home of the Universal," *The Universal Weekly*, 2 August 1913, p. 9.
13. "Feature Films," *The Universal Weekly*, 12 July 1913, pp. 15, 27.
14. "Feature Films," *The Universal Weekly*, 9 August 1913, p. 27.

15. Ibid, pp. 13–16 and review of *The Heart of the Jewess*, *The Moving Picture World*, 9 August 1913, p. 674.
16. "Feature Films," *The Universal Weekly*, 9 August 1913, p. 13.
17. Louis Reeves Harrison, review of *The Heart of the Jewess*, *The Moving Picture World*, 19 July 1913, p. 300.
18. "Scotch Irish Actress Triumphs in Jewish Role," *The Universal Weekly*, 6 September 1913, p. 8.
19. "Pathos and Romance in New Jewish Feature," *The Universal Weekly*, 27 September 1913, p. 13, and review of *Bleeding Hearts*, *The Moving Picture World*, 27 September 1913, p. 1424.
20. Review of *Bleeding Hearts*, *The New York Dramatic Mirror*, 8 October 1913, p. 30.
21. "'How the Jews Care for Their Poor,' New Imp Picture," *The Universal Weekly*, 25 October 1913, p. 8, and "How the Jews Care for Their Poor," *The Motion Picture World*, 18 October 1913, p. 272.
22. "Annual Banquet of Brooklyn Federation of Jewish Charities," *The Universal Weekly*, 13 December 1913, p. 17.
23. "Films Show Work of Jewish Charities," *The New York Times*, 6 April 1914, p. 18.
24. "A House of Feature Ideas," *The Moving Picture World*, 14 June 1913, p. 1142.
25. *Moving Picture World*, 29 November 1913, p. 1047.
26. "Mendel Beilis," *Variety*, 5 December 1913, p. 16.
27. Review of *Escaped from Siberia*, *The Moving Picture World*, 2 May 1914, p. 795.
28. Review of *Uriel Acosta*, *Variety*, 19 June 1914, p. 21.
29. "A Passover Miracle," *The Kalem Kalendar*, 15 March 1914, p. 3, and "Jewish Religious Subject," *The Moving Picture World*, 14 March 1914, p. 1369.
30. "News Items of the Kalem Players," *Kalem Kalendar*, 15 March 1914, p. 4.
31. Review of *A Passover Miracle*, *The New York Dramatic Mirror*, 1 April 1914, p. 30.
32. *The Jewish Independent* (Cleveland), 10 April 1914, p. 7.
33. Peter Milne, review of *Children of the Ghetto*, *The Motion Picture News*, 20 January 1915, p. 53, and review of *Children of the Ghetto*, *Motography* (Chicago), 6 March 1915, pp. 382–83.

## Chapter 3

1. Salo W. Baron, *The Russian Jew under Tsars and Soviets* (New York: Macmillan Publishing Co., 1976), p. 175.
2. Ibid., pp. 226–27.
3. Jay Leyda, "Between Explosions," *Film Quarterly*, Summer 1970, pp. 33–38.

NOTES 123

4. Jay Leyda, *Kino*, p. 136.
5. Information from Dr. Louis Cohen.
6. *Luftmench*, one who buys and sells air (dreams) and makes a living out of it.
7. *The Jewish Exponent* (Philadelphia), 4 October 1935, p. 14.
8. Ben-Ami Raiken, *Habima*, trans. A. H. Gross and I. Soref (New York: Thomas Yoseloff, 1957) pp. 142–144.
9. Walter Duranty, "Russian Moviedom Faces Real Tragedy," *The New York Times*, 24 March 1927, p. 7.
10. Isaac Babel, *Isaac Babel, The Lonely Years, 1925–1939*, trans. Andrew R. MacAndrew and Max Hayward, ed. Nathalie Babel (New York: Farrar, Straus & Co., 1964) pp. 72–73.
11. Isaac Babel, "Wandering Stars a Film Story," in *Isaac Babel: The Forgotten Prose*, ed. and trans. Nicholas Straud (Ann Arbor: Ardis, 1978) pp. 110–119.
12. Paul Babitsky and John Rimberg, *The Soviet Film Industry* (New York: Frederick A Praeger, 1955) p. 165.
13. Review of *Seeds of Freedom*, *The New York Times*, 9 September 1929, p. 10.
14. Review of *A Jew at War*, *The New York Times*, 25 July 1931, p. 11, and review of *A Jew at War*, *Motion Picture Herald*, 1 August 1931, p. 26.
15. Harry M. Rabinowicz, *The Legacy of Polish Jewry* (New York: Thomas Yoseloff, 1965) pp. 46–52.
16. Ibid., p. 156.
17. Zygmund Turkow, *Di Ibergerisene Tkufe: Fragmenten fun Mayn Lebn* [The Discontinued Period: Fragments from My Life] (Buenos Aires: Central Farband, 1961) p. 92.
18. Walter Fritz, *Die Österreichischen Spielfilme der Stummfilmzeit 1907–1930* [The Austrian Fiction Films of the Silent Film Era 1907–1930] (Vienna: Osterreichischen Filmarchivs, 1967).
19. Interview with Molly Picon, Jerusalem, Israel (date and interviewer unknown).
20. "Mazel Tov in Yiddish," *Variety*, 3 September 1924, p. 2.
21. Review of *The Jews in Poland*, *The New York Times*, 27 August 1920, p. 8.
22. "The Prompt Book," *The American Hebrew*, 26 February 1926, p. 497.
23. Review of *Broken Hearts*, *The New York Times*, 13 March 1926, p. 10, and *The Moving Picture World*, 20 March 1926, p. 184.

## Chapter 4

1. Cheavans, David, "Export Film Center Here," *The Telegraph* (New York), 4 August 1930.
2. "Negro and Yiddish Film Boom," *Variety*, 3 January 1940, p. 36.

3. Joseph Seiden, "Press Release," July 1948.
4. "Jewish Films in Own Tongue," *Variety*, 22 January 1930.
5. Joseph Seiden, "Press Release," July 1948. This may have been the old Talmadge studio.
6. Ibid.
7. Kenneth W. Munden, ed., *The American Film Institute Catalog, Feature Films 1921–1930* (New York: R. R. Bowker Co., 1971).
8. "Union Yiddish Actors Barred from Talkies," *Jewish Ledger* (Hartford, Conn.), 23 July 1930, and "Union Yiddish Actors Barred from Talkies," *The World* (Philadelphia), 1 July 1930.
9. "Judea Films Signs Two Yiddish Stars," *Exhibitors Daily Review and Motion Picture Today*, 22 March 1930.
10. "Compromise Settles Fight over Showing of Initial Yiddish Talkies in Tel Aviv," *Jewish Daily Bulletin*, 30 September 1930 and "Yiddish Film Starts Rioting in Palestine," *The World*, 28 September 1930.
11. Joseph Seiden, "Press Release," July 1941.
12. Jack Alicoate, ed., *The 1931 Film Daily Yearbook* (New York: J. E. Brulator, 1931), p. 230.
13. Joseph Seiden, "Press Release," July 1941.
14. "First Yiddish All Talking Picture Given Preview," *The Scribe* (Portland, Ore.), 12 September 1930, p. 6.
15. Review of *East Side Sadie*, *The Film Daily*, 2 June 1929, p. 3.
16. Advertisement for *The Eternal Prayer*, *The Detroit Jewish Chronicle*, 20 December 1929, p. 11.
17. "Movie: New York Notes," *Close-up*, February 1930, p. 98.
18. "'Joseph and His Brethren,' Jewish Talking Picture at Orchestra Hall," *Detroit Jewish Chronicle*, 11 April 1930, p. 9.
19. Nathan M. Kaganoff, Susan Landy, and Bruce Rosen, *Catalog of the Abram and Frances Pascher Kanof Collection of Yiddish Theatre and Motion Picture Posters* (Waltham, Mass.: American Jewish Historical Society, 1972).
20. Interview with Joseph Green, in New York City, 28 April 1976, conducted by the author.
21. Ibid.
22. Ibid.
23. Ibid.
24. "Yiddish Talking Picture at JCC," *Iowa Jewish News* (Des Moines), 10 November 1932, p. 4.
25. Review of *The Wandering Jew*, *Film Daily*, 21 October 1933, p. 4.
26. Troy, William, "Films, 'Marius' and Others," *The Nation*, 3 May 1933, p. 511, and review of *The Return of Nathan Becker*, *Motion Picture Herald*, 29 April 1933.
27. Advertising flyer for the Acme Theatre, New York, New York, 6 April 1935.

## Chapter 5

1. Maxwell Hamilton, "Movie Maker Joe Seiden Keeps 3-Room Studio Humming; Script for His Latest Epic Cost 20 Cents—And It's a Wow," *Brooklyn Daily Eagle*, 7 April 1936.
2. Ibid.
3. Interview with Harold Seiden, in Woodland Hills, California, 10 January 1977. Conducted by the author.
4. Interview with Leo Fuchs, by telephone, Los Angeles, California, 18 July 1976. Conducted by the author.
5. Ibid.
6. Morris Freedman, "Contemporary of William Fox Still Making Yiddish Films." *New York Herald Tribune*, 14 November 1948.
7. Interview with Harold Seiden.
8. Publicity material, Cinema Service Corporation.
9. Ibid.
10. Ibid.
11. Ibid.
12. Peter Bogdanovich, "Edgar G. Ulmer, An Interview," *Film Culture*, no. 58-50 (1974), p. 216. Pare Lorentz said this.
13. Ibid., p. 207. This was probably Joseph Green and *Yiddle with His Fiddle*.
14. Ibid., p. 208.
15. Ibid., p. 208.
16. Ibid., p. 210.
17. Ibid., p. 217.
18. Ibid., p. 218.
19. Ibid., p. 218.
20. Ibid., p. 214.
21. Ibid., p. 216.
22. Ibid., p. 217.
23. Review of *The Singing Blacksmith*, *Variety*, 9 November 1938, p. 17.
24. Interview with David Opatoshu, by telephone (Malibu, California), 3 November 1976. Conducted by the author.
25. Ibid.
26. Advertisement for *Americaner Shadchen*.
27. Review of *The Light Ahead*, *New York Times*, 23 September 1939, p. 22; *Box Office*, 7 October 1939, p. 29; *The Film Daily*, 12 October 1939, p. 5. This film has not been available for viewing for some time.
28. Advertisement for *The People Eternal*.
29. Review of *Tevya*, *New York Times*, 22 December 1939, p. 15.
30. Interview with David Opatoshu.
31. Jack Alicoate, ed., *The Film Daily Yearbook, 1939* (New York: J. E. Brulator, 1940).

32. Review of *Joseph in the Land of Egypt, Film Daily*, 22 May 1932, p. 5.
33. Review of *Tevya, New York Times*, 22 December 1939, p. 15.
34. Review of *Mirele Efros, Variety*, 25 October 1939, p. 23.
35. Review of *I Want to Be a Mother, New York Herald Tribune*, 1 March 1937, p. 9.
36. Review of *Motel the Operator, New York Times*, 16 January 1940, p. 9; review of *I Want to Be a Mother, The New York Herald Tribune*, 1 March 1937, p. 9.
37. "Cinema Theatre to be Opened at Jewish Center," *Kansas City Jewish Chronicle*, 2 December 1938, p. 1.

## Chapter 6

1. Interview with Joseph Green.
2. Interview with Molly Picon.
3. Review of *Yiddle with His Fiddle, Motion Picture Daily*, 5 January 1937, p. 3.
4. Interview with Joseph Green.
5. Ibid.
6. Ibid.
7. Ibid.
8. Ibid.
9. Review of *A Brivele der Mamen, New York Times*, 15 September 1939, p. 26.
10. Review of *A Brivele der Mamen, Motion Picture Daily*, 22 September 1939, p. 7.
11. Interview with Joseph Green.
12. Review of *Al Chet, Variety*, 15 September 1937, p. 15; *New York Times*, 9 September 1937, p. 19.
13. Jack Alicoate, ed., *Film Daily Yearbook* (New York: J. E. Brulator, 1943).

# Bibliography

### Books, Encyclopedias, and Yearbooks

Alicoate, Jack, ed. *The Film Daily Yearbook.* New York: J. E. Brulator, 1926–43.

Aroseve, Alexander Vokovlevich, ed. *Soviet Cinema.* Moscow: VOKS, 1935.

Isaac Babel. *The Forgotten Prose.* Edited and translated by Nicholas Stroud. Ann Arbor: Ardis, 1978.

———*Isaac Babel, The Lonely Years 1925–1939.* Translated by Andrew R. MacAndrew, and Max Hayward. Edited by Nathalie Babel. New York: Farrar, Straus & Co., 1964.

Babitsky, Paul, and Rinberg, John. *The Soviet Film Industry.* New York: Frederick A. Praeger, 1955.

Baron, Salo W. *The Russian Jew under Tsars and Soviets.* New York: Macmillan Publishing Co., 1976.

Burkos, Alexander S. *Soviet Cinema: Directors and Films.* Hamden, Conn.: Andon Books, 1976.

Copyright Office of Library of Congress. *Catalog of Copyright Entries Cumulative Series Motion Pictures 1912–1939.* Copyright Office of Library of Congress, 1951.

Den, David. *Svartz oyf Vays* [Black on White]. New York: Greenwich Printing, 1962.

*Encyclopaedia Judaica,* 1971 ed. S.v. "Austria," "Motion Pictures."

*Film Production der USSR 1931–32.* Berlin: 193?.

*Filmography Catalog of Jewish Films in Israel: The Abraham F. Rad Jewish Film Archives.* The Hebrew University of Jerusalem, The Institute of Contemporary Jewry, 1972.

Fox, Stuart. *Jewish Films in the United States: A Comprehensive Survey and Descriptive Filmography.* Boston: G. K. Hall & Co., 1976.

Glassman, Leo M., ed. *Biographical Encyclopedia of American Jews: 1935.* New York: Maurice Jacobs and Leo M. Glassman, 1935.

Glicksman, William M. *In the Mirror of Literature.* New York: Living Books, 1966.

Greenberg, Eliezer, and Howe, Irving. *A Treasury of Yiddish Stories.* New York: Schocken Books, 1974.

Hale, William Storm, and Minus, Johnny. *Film Superlist: 20,000 Motion Pictures in the Public Domain.* Hollywood: 7 Arts Press, 1973.

Hetty, Spiers, and Reed, Langford. *Who's Who in Filmland.* 3rd ed. London: Chapman & Hall, 1932.

Howe, Irving. *World of Our Fathers.* New York: Harcourt Brace Jovanovich, 1976.

Kaganoff, Nathan M.; Landy, Susan; and Rosen, Bruce. *Catalog of the Abram and Frances Pascher Kanof Collection of Yiddish Theater and Motion Picture Posters.* Waltham, Mass.: American Jewish Historical Society, 1972.

Lawerence, Jerome. *Actor: The Life and Times of Paul Muni.* New York: G. P. Putnam's Sons, 1974.

Lewis, Albert, ed. *Catalogue of the Stories and Plays Owned by Fox Film Corporation.* Los Angeles: Times-Mirror Press, 1931.

Leyda, Jay. *Kino: A History of the Russian and Soviet Film.* London: George Allen and Unwin, 1960.

Lifson, David. *The Yiddish Theatre in America.* New York: Thomas Yoseloff, 1965.

Martin, Marcel; Schnitze, Jean; and Schnitze, Luda, ed. *Cinema in Revolution, the Heroic Era of Soviet Film.* Translated by David Robinson. New York: Hill and Wang, 1973.

Miller James. *The Detroit Yiddish Theatre, 1920–1937.* Detroit: Wayne State University Press, 1967.

Munden, Kenneth W., ed. *The American Film Institute Catalog, Feature Films 1921–1930.* New York: R. R. Bowker Co., 1971.

*New Films Production of USSR.* Moscow: Intergorkino, 1933.

Nulman, Macy. *Concise Encyclopedia of Jewish Music.* New York: McGraw-Hill Book Co., 1975.

Picon, Molly. *Molly!* New York: Simon and Shuster, 1980.

Rabinowicz, Harry M. *The Legacy of Polish Jewry.* New York: Thomas Yoseloff, 1965.

Raiken, Ben-Ami. *Habima.* Translated by A. H. Gross and I. Soref. New York: Thomas Yoseloff, 1957.

Ramsey, Terry, ed. *International Motion Picture Almanac 1938–39.* New York: Quigley Publishing Co., 1938.

Sandrow, Nahama. *Vagabond Stars: A World History of the Yiddish Theatre.* New York: Harper & Row, 1977.

Spehr, Paul C. *The Movies Begin.* Dobbs Ferry: Morgan Press, 1977.

Taylor, Richard. *The Politics of the Soviet Cinema 1917–1929.* Cambridge: Cambridge University Press, 1979.

Toeplitz, Jerzy, gen. ed. *Historia Filmu Polskiego.* 3 vols. Warsaw: Wyadaunictwa Artystyczne i Filmowe, 1966. Vol. 1: *1895–1929,* by Wiadyslaw Banaskiewig and Witold Wilczak.

———. *Historia Stuki Filmoweg.* 3 vols. Warsaw: Filmowa Agencja Wydawnicza, 1955, 1956, 1967. Vol.1: *1895–1918.* Vol. 2: *1918–1928.* Vol. 3: *1934–1939.*

Turkow, Zygmund. *Di Ibergerisene Tkufe: Fragmenten Fun Mayn Lebn* [The Discontinued Period: Fragments From My Life]. Buenos Aires: Central Farband, 1961.

Walter, Fritz. *Die Österreichischen Spielfilm der Stummfilmzeit 1907–1930* [The Austrian Fiction Films of the Silent Film Era]. Vienna: Auftragendes Österreichischen Filmarchivs herausgegeben von der Österreichischer Gesellschaft für Filmwissenschaft.

Zylbercweig, Zalmen. *Lexicon of the Yiddish Theater.* Vols. 1–5. New York, Mexico City: Hebrew Actors Union of America, 1931, 1959, 1961, 1967.

## Magazines and Journals

Bakshy, Alexander. "Films: A Lesson from Moscow." *The Nation*, 25 June 1930, p. 650.

Bogdanovich, Peter. "Edgar G. Ulmer, An Interview." *Film Culture* 58, 59, 60 (1974): 206–235.

Bukowiecki, Leon. "Early Polish Films." *Films and Filming* (London), September 1958, p. 10.

Review of *The Dybbuk*, *Time*, 7 February 1938.

Erens, Patricia. "Mentshlekhakayat Conquers All; The Yiddish Cinema in America." *Film Comment*, January-February 1976, pp. 48–53.

Ford, Charles. "Russian Films before the Soviet." *Films in Review*, November 1953, pp. 472–74.

Goodman, Ezra. "Hollywood Is Worried." *Sight and Sound* (London), Autumn 1939, p. 106.

Hill, Steven P. "A Quantitative View of Soviet Cinema." *Cinema Journal*, Spring 1972, pp. 18–25.

Leyda, Jay. "Between Explosions." *Film Quarterly*, Summer 1970, pp. 33–38.

"Movie: New York Notes." *Close-up* 6, February 1930, p. 98.

"The Prompt Book," *The American Hebrew*, 26 February 1926, p. 497.

Rosenbaum, P. "The First Picture Show." *Film Comment*, March-April, 1975.

Troy, William. "Films: Marius and Others." *The Nation*, 3 March 1933, p. 511.

Vesello, Arthur: "Sacha Guitry and the Rest." *Sight and Sound*, Autumn 1939, p. 143.

## Newspapers

*The Albany Jewish Bulletin*, 1930.
*The Brooklyn Daily Eagle*, 1936.
*Der Tog* (New York), 1930–1940.
*The Detroit Jewish Chronicle*, 1929–1941.

*The Evening Telegram*, 1930.
*The Forward* (New York), 1930–1940.
*The Intermountain Jewish News* (Denver), 1930.
*The Iowa Jewish News* (Des Moines), 1932–1940.
*The Jewish Daily Bulletin*, 1930.
*The Jewish Exponent* (Philadelphia), 1930–1938.
*The Jewish Independent* (Cleveland), 1914–1941.
*The Jewish Ledger* (Hartford), 1930.
*The Jewish Tribune*, 1930.
*The Kansas City Jewish Chronicle*, 1930–1941.
*The New York American*, 1930.
*The New York Herald Tribune*, 1930–1948.
*The New York Times*, 1914–1980.
*The Scribe* (Portland), 1920–1938.
*The World*, 1930.

## Trade Papers

*The Bioscope* (London), 1913–1918.
*Boxoffice*, 1936–1951.
*The Cinema* (London), 1954.
*Cinematography* (New York), 1930.
*Exhibitors Daily Review and Motion Picture Today*, 1930.
*Exhibitors Herald World*, 1930.
*The Film Daily*, 1929–1950.
*The Film Index*, 1911.
*The Kalem Kalendar* (New York), 1914.
*Monthly Film Bulletin* (London), 1937–1971.
*The Motion Picture Daily*, 1937–1939.
*The Motion Picture Herald*, 1931–1936.
*The Motion Picture News*, 1915–1930.
*The Motion Picture Review Digest*, 1936–1939.

*Motography* (Chicago), 1914–1915.
*The Moving Picture World*, 1911–1926.
*The National Exhibitor*, 1937–1940.
*The New York Dramatic Mirror*, 1911–1914.
*Today's Cinema* (London), 1938.
*The Universal Weekly* (New York), 1913–1914.
*Variety*, 1913–1940.

## Other Reference Sources

New Hyde Park, New York. Private Collection of Harold Seiden.
New York, New York. Museum of the City of New York, Dazian Library of the Performing Arts.
New York, New York. Yiddish Scientific Institute Library.
Philadelphia, Pa. Gratz College, Music Library.
Waltham, Mass. Rutenberg and Everett Yiddish Film Library.

# Filmography

## Soviet Union

### *Features*

*The Beilis Case (Delo Beilisa).* 1917, 6 reels, silent.
 Director, Josef Soifer or Yevgeni Bauer; screenplay, N. Breshkov-Breskovsky, Y. Yakovlev; camera, N. Toporkov.
 CAST: Y. Yakovlev, Malkevich-Khodakovskaya, S. Kuznetsov

*Benya Krik.* Vufku, 1926, silent.
 Director, Vladimir Vilner; based on *The Odessa Tales* by Isaac Babel; screenplay, Isaac Babel.
 CAST: V. Shumski, M. Leorov.

*Beser dem Tot oder aza Shand (Better Death Than Shame).* 1914.
 CAST: N. B. Leonov.

*Birobidjan* (see *Seekers of Happiness*).

*The Bloody Jest (Der Blutiken Shpas).* 1917, silent.
 Director, Alexander Arkatov; screenplay, Alexander Arkatov, V. Voldo.

*A Brivele der Mamen (A Little Letter to Mother).* 1911.
 CAST: Smolenski.

*Cain and Artem.* Sovkino, 1929, 78 min., silent.
  Director, P. P. Petrov-Bytov; based on the novel by Maxim Gorky; camera, N. Wishakoff.
  CAST: Nikolai Simonov, Emit Gall, Yelena Yegorova, Georgy Uvarov.

*God of Vengeance.* Pathé Frères Moscow, 1912, 835 m., silent.
  Director, Alexander Arkatov; based on the play by Sholem Asch; plot, Georges Meyer (Joseph Mundviller); design, Cheslav Sabinsky.
  CAST: Israel Arko, Braginskya, Brandesco, Kundinskaya.

*A Greater Promise* (see *Seekers of Happiness*).

*If I Were Rothschild (Ven Ich Bin Roytshild).* 1918, silent.
  Screenplay, Alexander Arkatov from Sholom Aleichem.

*A Jew at War.* Ukrainfilm, 1931, silent.
  Director, Grigori Roshal; author and screenplay, Vera Stroyeva, S. Roshal; from *The Dreamer* by David Gorelick; camera, Michael Belsky; titles, Michael Gold.
  CAST: Venyamin Zuskin, S. Petrov, E. Pinikova, N. Lyanov, Mikola Nademsky, Semyon Svashenko, B. Shelestov-Zavz.

*The Jew on the Land.* 1927, silent.
  Director, Abram Room.

*Jewish Luck* (see *The Matchmaker*).

*Jewish Regiment (Evereisky Polk).* 1923, silent.
  Director, Gregory Gritcher (?).

*Judge, People.* 1918, silent.
  Director, Alexander Arkatov; screenplay, from the play by I. L. Peretz.

*Kiddish Hashem.* 1914.
  Producer, Reznikov.
  CAST: M. D. Fachler, R. Fachler.

*Lai Chyeim (Good Luck).* Pathé Frères Moscow, 1911, 4 reels, silent.

Director, Kai Hansen; plot, Georges Meyer; screenplay, Alexander Arkatov; design, Cheslav Sabinsky.
CAST: M. Reizen, Nikolai Vasiliev, L. Sychova, Mikhail Doronin.

*Laughter through Tears.* Vufku, 1928, 80 min., silent.
Director, Gregory Gritcher; based on *Mottele Peyse, The Cantor's Son*, by Sholom Aleichem; camera, Parkash, Borovsky, Vergio; editor, Joseph Burstyn; music, Sholem Secunda; sound effects, Al Harbuyer; English titles, Wolf Kaufman; narrator, Michael Rosenberg.
CAST: J. A. Kovenberg, A. D. Goritcheva, D. A. Cantor, M. D. Senelnikova, S. J. Silberman, A. J. Vubnik, F. A. Soslovsky, F. K. Silberman, M. L. Laur.
Sound added in 1933.

*Mabul.* Sovkino, 1926, silent.
Directors, Yevgeni Ivanov-Barkov, Boris Ilyitch Vershilov; based on *The Deluge* by Sholom Aleichem; screenplay, D. Rudenski, V. Popova-Khanzhonkova; adaptation, D. Rudenski; camera, Alphonse Winkler, A. Solodkov, G. Yegyazarov; design, R. Falk, Dmitri Kolupayev.
CAST: A. Dzuybiha, Ch. Efraiti, Benno Schneider, Tmima, Ben-Chayeem, A. Baratz, D. Itkin, Hannah Rovina, Nahum Zemach, E. Bertonov, I. Varshvaer, Raiken Ben-Ami, N. Viniar.

*The Matchmaker.* Goskino, 1925, 90 min., silent.
Director, Alexis Granowski; based on the *Menachem Mendel* stories by Sholom Aleichem; screenplay, Alexis Granowski; music Leo Pulver; camera, Edward Tisse, Vasili Khvatov, N. S. Strukov; design, Nathan Altman; assistant director, Gregory Gritcher.
CAST: Shlomo Mikhoels, Tamara Adelheim.
A.k.a. *Jewish Luck (Yiddishe Glikn).*

*Mirele Efros.* Moscow Gaumont, 1912, silent.

*Motel the Weaver (Motele Shpinder).* Vufku, 1928, 6,240 ft., silent.
Director, Vladimir Vilner; screenplay, Solomon Lazurin; camera, Boris Zavelyov.
CAST: M. Lorov, A. D. Goritcheva, Y. Mindler, J. A. Kovenberg, Y. Razman.

*The Return of Nathan Becker.* Belgoskino, 1933, 71 min.
Producer, Boris Shpis and R. M. Milman; directors, Boris Shpis and R. M. Milman; scenario, Peretz Markish; music, Brusilovski; camera, Mikhailov.
CAST: David Gutman, Shlomo Mikhoels, Elena Kashnitzkaya, Kador-Ben Selim, B. Babotchkin, V. Yoblonsky.

*Russian Father.* Ukrainfilm(?).

*Seeds of Freedom.* Belgoskino, 1929, silent.
Director, Grigori Roshal; author and screenplay, S. Roshal and Vera Stroyeva; camera, R. Kovlovski; titles, Shelly Hamilton.
CAST: J. Undershalk, Tamara Adelheim, A. Sandel, M. D. Senelnikova, A. Nechkev, A. Grinfield, Leonid M. Leonidoff.

*Seekers of Happiness.* Belgoskino, 1934.
Director, Vladimir Korsh-Sablin; screenplay, Johan Seitzer, G. Koberts; music, Isaac Dunayevsky; camera, S. Rayabov, K. Pogodin; design, V. Pokrovsky; codirector, I. Shapiro.
CAST: Maria Blumenthal-Tamarina, B. E. Zhukovsky, S. K. Yorov, L. M. Taits, L. A. Schmidt, N. K. Valyano, A. M. Karev, Ivrya Brodsky, Venyamin Zuskin.
A.k.a. *Birobidjan, A Greater Promise.*

*Sorrows of Sarah.* Khanzhonkov, 1913, 800 m.
Director, Alexander Arkatov; screenplay, Volberg; camera, Alexander Rillo.
CAST: T. Shornikova, A. Bibikov, P. Maximova, Ivan Mozhukhin, V. Turzhansky.

*Vu Iz Mein Hasa? (Where Is My Khasa?).* Gaumont Moscow, 1912.
CAST: S. L. Akanski.

*Wandering Stars.* Vufku, 1926, silent.
Director, Gregory Gritcher; based on the story by Sholom Aleichem; screenplay, Isaac Babel.

*The War and the Jew.* Mizrakh, 1914, silent.
Screenplay, I. Tenerama.
CAST: G. M. Kalik-Gramov.
Sound added in 1915.

# FILMOGRAPHY

### Shorts

*Puppets,* 1935.
Yosel Cutler and his puppets.

## Poland

### Features

*Fiction*

*Al Chet (I Have Sinned).* Warsaw Art Productions, 1938, 93 min.
   Director, Shaul Goskind; camera, Stanislaw Lipinski; music, Henryk Kon.
   CAST: Rachel Holzer, Abraham Morevsky, Shimon Dzigan, Israel Schumacher, Kurt Katch, Ruth Turkow, Herbert Scherzer, Charles Buzgan.

*Bigamistka* (see *Zajn Wajbs Man*).

*Bóg, Człowiek I Szatan* (see *God, Man and Devil*).

*A Brivele der Mamen (A Little Letter to Mother).* Greenfilm, 1937.
   Producer and director, Joseph Green; screenplay, M. Osherwitz and Joseph Green; music, Abe Ellstein; camera, Seweryn Steinwurzel; editor, J. M. Neuman; titles, Julian Leigh.
   CAST: Lucy Gehrman, Alexander Stein, Isaac Grudberg, Irving Bruner, Gertrude Bulman, Chane Levin, Max Bozhyk, Edmund Zayenda, Mischa Gehrman, Simche Fostel, Samuel Landau.

*Dem Chazons Tochter (The Cantor's Daughter).* Kosmofilm, 1913, 960 m., silent.
   Director, Stanislaw Sebel; based on the play by Zalmen Libin.
   CAST: Samuel Landau, Regina Kaminska, Sonia Szlosberg, Szaja Rotsztejn.
A.k.a. *Córka Kantora.*

*Córka Kantora* (see *Dem Chazons Tochter*).

*A Daughter of Her People* (see United States, *A Daughter of Her People*).

*The Dybbuk.* Fencke Films, 1938, 122 min.
Director, Michael Wasynski; based on the play by S. Anski; screenplay, Al. Kacyzna, Mark Arenstein; music, Henryk Kon; ritual songs, Chief Cantor Gerson Sirota; camera, Albert Wywerka; design, Alexander Marten; editor, George Roland; choreography, Judith Berg; historical research, Dr. Meyer Balaban; interpretation, Jacob Mestel; titles, Leonora Fleischer; translation, Abraham Armband.
CAST: Abraham Morevsky, R. Samberg, Moishe Lipman, Lili Liliana, Dina Halpern, Gerszon Lamberger, Leon Liebgold, Max Bozhyk, Samuel Landau, S. Bronecki, M. Messinger, Z. Katz, Abram Kurc, David Lederman.

*Di Fersztoyśene (The Disinherited).* Sila, 1912, 1000 m., silent.
Director, Stanislaw Sebel; screenplay, E. Waksman.
A.k.a. *Wydziedziczeni.*

*God, Man and Devil.* Sila, 1912, 550 m., silent.
Director, Stanislaw Sebel; based on the play by Jacob Gordin.
CAST: Rudolf Zaslawski.
A.k.a. *Bóg, Człowieck i Szatan.*

*Gots Sztrof (God's Punishment).* Kosmofilm, 1913, 900 m., silent.
Director, Stanislaw Sebel; based on the play by Jacob Gordin.
CAST: Regina Kaminska, Samuel Landau, Tea Izraelis, Helen Gotlib, Mark Mejerson, Aron Polakow, Herman Wajsman, Ida Kaminska, Jakub Libert.
A.k.a. *Kara Boža.*

*Hasa die Yesome (Hasa the Orphan).* Silent.
Director, Nahum Lipovski.
CAST: Esther Lipovski.

*Hasa die Yesome (Hasa the Orphan).* 1912, silent.
Director, Mark Arenstein.
CAST: Vilna Circle Theater.

*Herecle Mejuches.* Kosmofilm, 1913, 1500 m., silent.
Director, Stanislaw Sebel; screenplay, Moshe Richter.
CAST: Samuel Landau, Regina Kaminska, Herman Wajsman, Isaac Samdberg, Leszko, Herman Fiszelewicz.

*Jeden Z 36* (see *Der Lamedvovnik*).

*Jolly Paupers (Freyliche Kabtsonim)*. Sektor, 1938, 62 min.
Producers, Itzhak and Shaul Goskind; director, Leon Fencke (?); screenplay, Itzak Manger.
CAST: Max Bozhyk, Shimon Dzigan, Israel Schumacher, Menasha Oppenheim, Zygmund Turkow, Ruth Turkow.

*Kara Boža* (see *Gots Sztrof*).

*Der Lamedvovnik*. Leo-Forbert Films, 1925, silent.
Director, Henry Szaro; screenplay, Henryk Bojm; camera, Seweryn Steinwurzel; design, Ferdinand Vlassak, M. Weintraub, A. Tenenbaum.
CAST: Jonas Turkow, Moishe Lipman, Helen Gotlib, Irma Gren, Klara Segalowicz, Alexander Maniecki, Michal Halicz, Chaim Sandler, Joseph Zaremba, K. Janowski.
A.k.a. *Jeden Z 36 (One of the 36)*.

*Leybe der Shuster (Leybe the Shoemaker)*. Silent.
Screenplay, from Prywski.
CAST: Warsaw Jewish Theater.

*Macocha* (see *Disztifmuter*).

*Małzenstwona Rozdrozu* (see *Zajn Wajbs Man*).

*Mamele (Little Mother)*. Greenfilm, 1938, 100 min.
Producer, Joseph Green; directors, Joseph Green and Konrad Tom; story, Meyer Schwartz and Konrad Tom; music, Abe Ellstein; camera, Seweryn Steinwurzel.
CAST: Molly Picon, Edmund Zayenda, Max Bozhyk, Gertrude Bulman, Simche Fostel, Menasha Oppenheim, Ola Shifko, Max Pearlman, Ruth Turkow, Lew Schriftzecer, Carl Latowich.

*Masters and Workers*. Mintus Company, 1912, silent.
Screenplay, from Tolstoy.
CAST: Mischa Fishzon.

*Mirele Efros*. Sila, 1912, 1030 m., silent.
Director, Stanislaw Sebel; based on the play by Jacob Gordin.
CAST: Regina Kaminska, Esther Rachel Kaminska, Rudolf Zaslawski, Ida Kaminska, David Lui, Herman Wajsman, Jakub Libert,

Sonia Edelman, Julius Adler, Avrom Yitskok Kaminsky, Tania Tetelbaum.

*Neighbors.* Best Films, 1938, 88 min.
Director, Leon Trystan; story, J. Fethke, N. Sondek; dialogue, Joseph Tunkel; songs, Henry Wars; art direction, Jacek Rotmil, Stephan Norris.
CAST: Helen Gross, Joseph Orwid, Eugene Bodo, L. Sempolinsky, The Warsaw Art Theater.
A.k.a. *Piętro Wyżej (The Apartment Above).*

*Nieznajomy* (see *Der Unbekanter*).

*Okrutny Ojciec* (see *Der Vilder Fater*).

*Piętro Wyżej* (see *Neighbors*).

*Dos Pintele Yid.* Mintus Company, 1914, silent.
Director, A. Slavinsky; screenplay, Boris Thomashevsky and Moishe Zeifert; camera, A. Slavinsky.

*[In the] Polish Woods (W Lasach Polskich).* Leo Forbert, 1929, silent.
Director, Jonas Turkow; based on the novel by Josef Opatoshu; screenplay, Henryk Bojm; camera, Ferdinand Vlassak; art director Leo Forbert.
CAST: Dina Blumenfeld, Silven Rich, Moishe Lipman, S. Prisament, Helen Gotlib, A. Ajzenberg, M. B. Sztejn, A. Rotman, D. Szajewicz, Tadeusz Wesolowski, Samuel Landau, Rosa Szoszara, J. Vermont, Alexander Maniecki, David Lederman, Anna Rapel, Chaim Sandler, I. Grabowska, Jacob Kurlender, A. Bozenski, Esther Rachel Kaminska, Jerzy Leszczyński, Klara Segalowicz, Luba Ditris.

*Der Purimspieler (The Jester).* Greenfilm, 1937, 83 min.
Producer, Joseph Green; directors, Joseph Green and Jan-Nowina Przybilski; screenplay, Joseph Victos; music, Nicholas Brodsky; camera, Seweryn Steinwurzel.
CAST: Miriam Kressyn, Zygmund Turkow, Hymie Jacobson, Isaac Samberg, Max Bozhyk, Berta Litwina, Eni Litan, Maka Bryn, Samuel Landau, Jakub Fiszer.

*Shma Yisroel.* Mintus Company, 1914, silent.
Director, Avrom Yitskhok Kaminsky; screenplay, from the play by Ossip Dymov.

*The Slaughter* (see *Di Szchite*).

*Di Szchite.* Kosmofilm, 1913, 900 m., silent.
Director, Stanislaw Sebel; based on the play by Jacob Gordin.
CAST: S. Adler, H. Kaminska.
A.k.a. *Ubŏj, The Slaughter.*

*Di Sztifmuter (The Stepmother).* Kosmofilm, 1914, 1600 m., silent.
Director, Stanislaw Sebel; based on the play by Jacob Gordin.
CAST: Aba Kompaneyets, M. Szlossberg, A. Ajzenberg, Szaja Rotsztejn, Samuel Landau, Herman Fiszelewicz.
A.k.a. *Macocha.*

*Tkijes Khaf (The Vow).* Leo-Forbert, 1924 (see United States, *Vilna Legend*).

*Ubŏj* (see *Di Szichte*).

*Der Unbekanter (The Stranger).* Kosmofilm, 1913, 1000 m., silent.
Director, Stanislaw Sebel; based on the play by Jacob Gordin.
CAST: Regina Kaminska, Wiera Zaslawska, Herman Wajsman, Jakub Libert.
A.k.a. *Nieznajomy.*

*Der Vilder Fater (The Cruel Father).* Sila, 1911, 1250 m., silent.
Director, Alexander Marten; based on the play by Jacob Gordin; camera, Stanislaw Sebel.
CAST: Zina Goldsztein, Herman Sieracki.
A.k.a. *Okrutny Ojciec.*

*The Vow.* Foreign Cinema Arts, 1938, 88 min.
Director, Henry Szaro; screenplay, Henryk Bojm.
CAST: Zygmund Turkow, Kurt Katch, E. Perlman, Isaac Grudberg, Moishe Lipman, Berta Litwina, Dina Halpern, Samuel Landau, Menasha Oppenheim, Max Bozhyk, Simche Fostel.

*Without a Home (Ahn a Heim).* Sektor, 1939, 88 min.
  Producer, Adolph Mann; director, Alexander Marten; based on the play by Jacob Gordin; music, O. Szajewez; camera, Janilowicz.
  CAST: Ida Kaminska, Alexander Marten, Dora Fakel, Irma Gren, Shimon Dzigan, Israel Schumacher, Ben Zucker.

*Wydziedziczeni* (see *Di Fersztoyśene*).

*Der Yeshiva Bocher.* Mintus Company, 1914, silent.
  Director, A. Slavinsky; screenplay, from the play by Isidore Zolatorefsky; camera, A. Slavinsky.

*Yiddle with His Fiddle (Yiddle mit'n Fiddle).* Greenfilm, 1937, 80 min.
  Producer, Joseph Green; director, Joseph Green and Jan-Nowina Przybilski; screenplay, Joseph Green; music, Abe Ellstein; lyrics, Itzik Manger; art direction, Jacob Kalich.
  CAST: Molly Picon, Simche Fostel, Max Bozhyk, Leon Liebgold, Dora Fakel, Samuel Landau, C. Lewin.
English version: *Castles in the Air.*

*Yom Hachupa (The Wedding Day).* Mintus Company, 1914, silent.
  Director, A. Slavinsky; screenplay, from the play by Jacob Gordin; camera, A. Slavinsky.

*Zajn Wajbs Man (His Wife's Man).* Kosmofilm, 1913, 1200 m., silent.
  Director, Stanislaw Sebel; screenplay, Majzela.
  CAST: Wiera Zaslawska, Israel Arko, Mischa Fishzon, Isaac Samberg, Helen Gotlib, Ida Kaminska.
A.k.a. *Bigamistka.*

*Zajn Wajbs Man (His Wife's Man).* 1916, silent.
  Based on *Zajn Wajbs Man* by Majzela.
  CAST, Isaac Samberg, Klonska, Ida Kaminska, Helen Gotlib, Samuel Landau, Kurz Rotberg, Szajwicz.
A.k.a. *Małzenstwona Rozdrozu.*

*Zvay Musicanten (Two Musicians).* 79 min.
  CAST: Helen Gross, Warsaw Art Players.

## Documentaries

*Children Must Laugh* (see *Mir Kumen On*).

*Jews in Poland* 1957.
Producers, Simon Federman and the Polish State Film Studios; director, B. Ladowicz; screenplay, A. Tadziemec.

*Mir Kumen On (We Arrive).* Sektor, 1937, 1300 m.
Director, Alexander Ford; screenplay, Joseph Pat, Moshe Lipschutz, S. Mendelsohn, H. S. Kazdan, Wanda Wasilevska; music, Henryk Kon, Yankel Trowpianski.
A.k.a. *Children Must Laugh.*

*Mirelebn Gerleben (We Live Again).*
Director, Nathan Gross.

*Unzere Kinder (Our Children).* 1949.
Producers, Shaul Goskind and Joseph Goldberg; director, Nathan Gross; screenplay, Rokhi Auerbach, music, Shaul Berezovsky, camera, Stanislaw Lipinski.
CAST: Shimon Dzigan, Israel Schumacher, Neumiah Gold.
Released 1951.

## Shorts

*City in Poland.* Contemporary, post–World War II.

*Sing Molly Sing.* Greenfilm.
Producer, Joseph Green.
CAST: Molly Picon.

*Zvay Musicanten (Two Musicians).*
CAST: Helen Gross, Warsaw Art Players.

## Austria

*Das Judenmädel (The Jewish Girl).* Helio Film or Ekran-Film, 1921, 1 reel, silent.
Director, Otto Kreisler; camera, Steffan Loront.
CAST: Molly Picon, Ferdinand Bonn, Franz Kammauf.

*Mazel Tov (Good Luck).* Listo-Film/Picon Film, 1923, 2380 m., 8 reels, silent.
Director, Sidney Goldin.
CAST: Molly Picon, Jacob Kalich, Eugen Neufelf, Johannes Roth.
A.k.a. *Ost und West (East and West).*

*Ost und West* (see *Mazel Tov*).

*Thou Shalt Remember* (see Yiskor).

*Yiskor.* Judische-Kunstfilm, 1924, 2511m., silent.
Producer, (U.S.) Penser & Goldberg; director, Sidney Goldin.
CAST: Maurice Schwartz, Oskar Beregi, Karl Götz, Dagny Servaes, Fran Abromowitz.
A.k.a. *Thou Shalt Remember (Gedenket . . . ).*

## United States

### *Features*

*Fiction*

*Americaner Shadchen (The American Matchmaker).* Fame Films, 1940, 93 min.
Producer and director, Edgar G. Ulmer; screenplay, S. Castle; story, G. Hamo; dialogue, S. Pressler; music, Sam Morgenstern; lyrics, William Mercur; camera, J. Burgi Cotner, Edward Hyland; art, William Saulter.
CAST: Judith Abarbanol, Rosetta Bialis, Leo Fuchs, Yudel Dubinsky, William Mear, Abraham Lax.

*Avram Ovenu* (see *The Eternal Jew*).

*Bar Mitzvah.* S & L Film Company, 1935, 85 min.
Director, Henry Lynn; based on the play by Boris Thomashevsky.
CAST: Boris Thomashevsky, Regina Zuckerberg, Peter Graf, Gertrude Bulman, Anita Chages, Leah Noemi, Sam Colton, Benny Schetmen, Morris Tarlowsky.

*The Black 107.* Ruby Features, 1913, 3 reels, silent.
Producer, Lewis J. Rubenstein; director, Sidney Goldin.
CAST: Jan Smoelski.

*Bleeding Hearts or Jewish Freedom under King Casimir of Poland.*
Victor Film Co., Universal-Imp, 1913, 3 reels, silent.
Producer, Mark Dintenfass; director, Sidney Goldin.
CAST: Irene Wallace, David Barantz, Harold Vosbaum.

*Broken Hearts.* Jaffe Art Films, 1926, 8 reels, silent.
Director, Maurice Schwartz; based on the play by Z. Libin; adaptation, Frances Taylor Patterson; camera, Frank Zukor.
CAST: Maurice Schwartz, Lila Lee, Wolf Goldfadden, Bina Abramowitz, Isidor Cashier, Anna Appel, Charles Nathanson, Liza Silbert, Theodore Silbert, Miriam Elias, Morris Strassberg, Henrietta Schmitzer, Betty Ferkauf, Louis Hyman, Leonid Snegoff, Julius Adler.
Released 1934 with music as *The Unfortunate Bride of Suffolk Street.*

*The Cantor's Son.* Eron Pictures, 1937, 90 min.
Producers, Arthur Block and Max Segal; director, Illya Motyleff; screenplay, Louis Freeman; dialogue, Mark Schweid; music, Alexander Olshanetsky; camera, Frank Zukor; editor, Leonard Weiss; titles, Julian Leigh.
CAST: Moishe Oysher, Florence Weiss, Judith Abarbanol, Michael Rosenberg, Isidor Cashier, Judah Bleich, Berta Guttenberg, Irving Honigman, Rose Wallerstein, Vicki Marcus, Lorraine Abarbanol.

*Catskill Honeymoon.* Pictorial Ventures, 1950, 93 min.
Producers, Martin Cohen and Jack LaMont; director, Joseph Berne; dialogue, Joel Jacobson; music arranged and conducted by Hymie Jacobson; camera, Charles Down; editors, Jack Kemp and Cy Brownstein; sound, Edward Fenton.
CAST: Michael Michalesko, Jan Bart, Bas Sheva, Bobby Colt, Henrietta Jacobson, Julius Adler, Mary La Roche, David and Dorothy Paige, Irving Grossman, Dina Goldberg, Max and Rose Bozhyk, Cookie Bowers, Mike Hammer.

*Der Chazon* (see *Overture to Glory*).

*The Children of the Ghetto.* Box Office Attraction Company, William Fox, 1915, 5 reels, silent.
Producer and director, Frank Powell; based on the novel by Israel Zangwill; screenplay, Edward Jose.
   CAST: Ethel Kaufman, Ruby Hoffman, David Bruce, William R. Hatch, Wilton Lackaye, Irene Boyle, Frank Andrews, Lewis Alberni.

*A Daughter of Her People.* 1933, 75 min.
   Based on the play by Judith Trachtenburg.
   CAST (silent): Vilna Troupe.
   CAST (sound): Joseph Greenberg, Michael Rosenberg, Ben Bosenko, Chaim Shnayer, Mischa Dorf, Helen Blay, Jacob Mestel, Paul Anderer.
Recut silent Polish film.

*A Dudele (A Home Spun Melody).* No release.
   Director, Joseph Seiden.

*East Side Sadie.* Worldart Film Co., 1929, 6 reels, silent.
   Director, Sidney Goldin; story, Sidney Goldin; screenplay, Isidore Frankel; music, Sholem Secunda; camera, Frank Zukor; editor, Sam Citen; titles, Sam Citen.
   CAST: Bertina Goldin, Machivinko, Mark Schweid, Abe Sinkoff, Jack Holliday, Jack Ellis, Boris Rosenthal, Lucia Backus.
Also sound version.

*Eli, Eli.* Cinema Service Corporation, 1940, 89 min.
   Director, Joseph Seiden; screenplay, Isidore Frankel; music, Sholem Secunda.
   CAST: Esther Feld, Lazar Freed, Irving Jacobson, Mae Schoenfeld, Muni Serebroff, Rose Greenfield, Max Baden, Paula Lubeska, Eddie Friedlander, David Yanover, Yetta Zwerling.

*Escaped from Siberia.* Great Players Feature Film Company, 1914, 5 reels, silent.
   Director, Sidney Goldin.

*Eternal Fools.* Judea Films, 1930.
   Director, Sidney Goldin; author, screenplay, dialogue, Harry Kalmanowitz; camera, Charles Levine, Sam Rosen; editor, Louis

Schwartz; recording engineer, Douglas Shearer.
CAST: Yudel Dubinsky, Judah Bleich, Bella Gudinsky, Seymour Rechtzeit, Isadore Metzer, Charlotte Goldstein, Beatrice Miller, Eddie Friedlander, Gertrude Krause.

*The Eternal Jew.* Jewish Talking Pictures Company, 1931, 62 min.
Supervisor, Sam Rosen; director, George Roland; author, Abraham Armband.
CAST: Cantor Leibele Waldman, Morris B. Samuylov, Rubin Wendrof, Celina Breenes.
Contains footage from *A Story of the Bible.*
A.k.a. *Avram Ovenu (Father Abraham).*

*The Eternal Prayer (Ad Mosae).* Metropolitan Studios, 1929, 36 min.
Producer, Max Cohen; director, Sidney Goldin; music, Abe Ellstein; lyrics, David Meyerovitch.
CAST: Lucy Levine, Anna Appel, Mark Schweid, Lazar Freed, Schmulikel.

*God, Man and Devil.* Aaron Films Corporation, 1950, 103 min.
Director, Joseph Zeiden (Seiden); based on the play by Jacob Gordin; screenplay, Isidore Frankel; music, Sholem Secunda.
CAST: Michael Michalesko, Gustav Berger, Berta Gersten, Esta Salzman, Shifra Lehrer, Max Bozhyk, Leon Schachter, Lucy Gehrman, Joshua Zeldis.

*The Great Advisor (Der Groyseretz Gever).* Cinema Service Corporation, 1940, 76 min.
Director, Joseph Seiden.
CAST: Irving Jacobson, Yetta Zwerling, Sol Dickstein, Max Baden, Muni Serebroff, Abraham Lax, Jacob Zanger, Rose Greenfield, Mae Schoenfeld, Isidore Frankel, Herman Rosen.

*Green Fields (Greene Felder).* Collective Film Producers, 1937, 110 min.
Executive Producer, Roman Rebush; directors, Edgar G. Ulmer and Jacob Ben-Ami; author, Peretz Hirschbein; screenplay, George G. Moskov; score, Vladimir Horowitz; camera, William Miller, J. Burgi Cotner; editor, Jack Kemp.
CAST: Michael Goldstein, Helen Beverly, Isidor Cashier, Anna

Appel, Max Vodney, Leah Noemi, Dena Drute, Saul Levine, Herschel Bernardi, Aron Ben-Ami.

*Happy Times* (see *Live and Laugh*).

*The Heart of a Jewess.* Victor Film Company, Universal-Imp, 1913, 2 reels, silent.
  Producer, Mark Dintenfass; director Sidney Goldin.
  CAST: Irene Wallace.

*Her Second Mother.* Cinema Service Corporation, 1941, 89 min.
  Director, Joseph Seiden; music, Sholem Secunda.
  CAST: Esta Salzman, Muni Serebroff, Yetta Zwerling, Jacob Zanger, David Lubritsky, Max Baden, Rose Greenfield, Seymour Rechtzeit, Isidore Frankel, Herman Rosen.

*The Holy Oath.* Cinema Service Corporation, 68 min.
  Music, Jack Stillman.
  CAST: Murray White, Anna Appel, Lazar Freed, Anna Weissman, Morris Strassberg, Lucy Levine.

*I Want to Be a Mother.* Jewish Talking Pictures Company, 1937, 84 min.
  Director, George Roland; story, Isidore Lash; camera, Joseph Freeman; sound, Murray Dichter.
  CAST: Moishe Feder, Rose Greenfield, Esta Salzman, Leo Fuchs, Hannah Hollander, Yetta Zwerling, Muni Serebroff, David Lubritsky, Sam Gertler, Cantor Leibele Waldman.

*A Jew in Exile* (see *The Wandering Jew*).

*The Jewish Melody.* Cinema Service Corporation, 1941, 89 min.
  Director, Joseph Seiden; music, Sholem Secunda.
  CAST: Isidor Cashier, Lazar Freed, Chaim Tauber, Seymour Rechtzeit, David Lubritsky, Jacob Zanger, Moishe Feder, Yetta Zwerling, Esta Salzman, Rose Greenfield, Mae Schoenfeld, Paula Klider.
A.k.a. *The Jewish Song*.

*The Jewish Song* (see *The Jewish Melody*).

*Joseph and His Brethren.* 1930.
Director, Adolph Gartner.

*Joseph in the Land of Egypt.* Guaranteed Picture Company, Inc., 1932.
Director, George Roland; adaptation and dialogue, Michael Goldberg; music, I. J. Hochman; editor, Jean Roland; recording engineer, Lyman J. Wiggin.
CAST: Ben Adler, Joseph Greenberg, Sigmund Zuckerberg, Herman Serotsky, Wolf Goldfadden, Joseph Schwartzberg, Wolf Barzell, Ida Adler, Gertrude Levitan, Sonya Adler.

*Di Klatshe* (see *The Light Ahead*).

*Kol Nidre.* Cinema Service Corporation, 1939, 89 min.
Director, Joseph Seiden; author, Ben Gitlitz; music, Sholem Secunda.
CAST: Cantor Leibele Waldman, Joel Felig Double Choir, Yetta Zwerling, Leon Liebgold, Lili Liliana, Menasha Oppenheim, Bertha Hart, David Lederman, Joseph Schoengold.

*Der Lebediker Yusem* (see *My Son*).

*The Light Ahead.* Ultra Films, 1939, 110 min.
Producer and director, Edgar G. Ulmer; based on the novels *Fishke der Krumer* and *Di Klatshe* by Mendele Mocher Sforim; adaptation and dialogue, Chaver Paver; camera, William Miller, J. Burgi Cotner; makeup, Eddie Senz.
CAST: Isidor Cashier, Helen Beverly, David Opatoshu, Yudel Dubinsky, Rosetta Bialis, Tillie Rabinowitz, Misha Fishman, Leon Seidenberg, Anne Guskin, Wolf Mercur, Jenny Cashier.
A.k.a. *Di Klatshe.*

*Live and Laugh.* Jewish Talking Pictures Company, Inc., 1933, 60 min.
Director, Max Wilner; author Max Wilner; editor, Sam Rosen; recording engineer, Murray Dichter.
CAST: Cantor Yossele Rosenblatt, Menasha Skulnick, Joseph Buloff, Pincus Lavenda, Seymour Rechtzeit, Yudel Dubinsky, Boris Rosenthal, Hymie Jacobson, Jack Shargel, Eddie Friedlander, Meyer Machtenburg, Chaim Tober, Max Wilner, Sadie Banks, Mae Simon.
A.k.a. *Happy Times.*

*The Living Orphan* (see *My Son*).

*Love and Sacrifice (Liebe un Leidenschaft)*. Jewish Talking Pictures Company, 1936, 75 min.
Director, George Roland; based on the novel *Love and Passion* by Isadore Zolatarefsky; screenplay, Joseph Seiden; music, Abe Schwartz.
CAST: Lazar Freed, Rose Greenfield, Cantor Leibele Waldman, Anna Thomashevsky, Louis Kramer, Morris Silber, William Schwartz, Esta Salzman.

*Mazel Tov Yidden (Congratulations, Jews)*. Cinema Service Corporation, 89 min.
CAST: Michael Rosenberg, Cantor Leibele Waldman, Sholem Secunda, Alexander Olshanetsky, Hannah Hollander, Esta Salzman, Anna Thomashevsky.

*Mirele Efros*. Credo Pictures, 1939, 87 min.
Producer, Roman Rebush; director, Joseph Berne; based on the play by Jacob Gordin; screenplay, Ossip Dymov and Joseph Berne; music, Vladimir Heifetz; editor, Leslie Vidor; art director, Sam Corse; production manager, George Moskov; sound engineer, Edwin Schabehar; assistant director, Louis Brandt; costumes, Madame Anna Kay; titles, Julien Leigh; technical advisor, Jacob Mestel; special assistant, Louis Jacobs.
CAST: Berta Gersten, Michael Rosenberg, Ruth Elbaum, Albert Lipton, Sara Krohner, Moishe Feder, Louis Brandt, Paula Walter, Jerry Rosenberg, Ella Brouner, Rubin Wendroff, Jacob Mestel, Moishe Schorr, Eugene Sigaloff, Clara Deutschmann.

*Monticello Here We Come*. Cinema Service Corporation, 1950, 83 min.
Producer and director, Joseph Seiden.
CAST: Menasha Skulnick, Joseph Buloff, Leo Fuchs, Max Wilner, Mary Forest, Joseph Bozhyk, Yetta Zwerling, Michael Rosenberg.

*Motel the Operator*. Cinema Service Corporation, 1940, 89 min.
Producer and director, Joseph Seiden; based on the novel by Sholom Aleichem; screenplay, Chaim Tauber; music, Sholem Secunda; camera, Don Malkomes, Charles Levine.
CAST: Chaim Tauber, Yetta Zwerling, Seymour Rechtzeit, Joseph Schoengold, Melvina Rappel, Jacob Zanger, Bertha Hart,

Maurice Krohner, Herman Rosen, Gertrude Krause, Isidore Frankel, Cantor Leibele Waldman, Joel Felig Double Choir.

*Mothers of Today.* Apex Productions, 1939, 95 min.
Director, Henry Lynn; story, Simon Wolf; screenplay, Henry Lynn.
CAST: Esther Feld, Max Rosenblatt, Gertrude Krause, Simon Wolf, Leon Seidenberg, Paula Lubelska, Vera Lubov, Arthur Winters, Louis Goldstein, Jack Shargel.

*My Son.* Jewish Talking Pictures Company, 1939, 90 min.
Director, Joseph Seiden; authors, Chaim Tauber, Joseph Seiden.
CAST: Gustav Berger, Fannie Rubina, Jerry Rosenberg, Harry Feld, Yetta Zwerling, Alexander Olshanetsky, Muni Berger, Ida Dworkin, Jacob Zanger.
A.k.a. *Der Lebediker Yusem, The Living Orphan.*

*My Yiddishe Mama.* Judea Films, 1930, 60 min.
Director, Sidney Goldin; author, Isadore Lillian.
CAST: Mae Simon.

*Nihilist Vengeance.* Victor Film Company, Universal-Imp, 1913, 2 reels, silent.
Director, Sidney Goldin.
CAST: Irene Wallace.

*Overture to Glory.* Elite Productions, 1940, 87 min.
Producers, Ludwig Lande, Ira Greene; associate producer, Sam Rosen; production supervisor, A. Weiss; director, Max Nosseck; screenplay, Ossip Dymov, J. Gladstone, L. Jones; music, Alexander Olshanetsky; camera, Sam Rosen; sound, Kay Ash.
CAST: Moishe Oysher, Benjamin Fishbein, Helen Beverly, Florence Weiss, Baby Winkler, Maurice Krohner, Lazar Freed, Jack Mylong Munz, Leonard Elliot, Lubar Wesoly, Ossip Dymov, Erika Zaranova, Ivan Busatt.
A.k.a. *Der Chazon.*

*A Passover Miracle.* Kalem, 1914, 2 reels, silent.
Screenplay, Benjamin Bardoness; technical supervisor, Shalom Masimon.
CAST: Henri Leone, Samuel Lowett, Irene Boyle, Irene Von Muller, Stephen Purdee.

*A People Eternal.* Six Star Production, 1939, 66 min.
   Director, Henry Lynn.
   CAST: Conrad Veidt, Peggy Ashcroft, Basil Bill, Marie Nevy, Ann Grey.
   YIDDISH DIALOGUE CAST: Ben Adler, Zena Goldstein, Leon Schechter, Lillian Bloom, Max Rosenblatt.
   Cut from *The Wandering Jew.* Twickenham Film Studios, 1935.

*The Power of Life.* Lynn Production, Inc., 1938, 92 min.
   Producer and director, Henry Lynn; author and screenplay, Isadore Zolatarefsky.
   CAST: Michael Michalesko, Morris Strassberg, Charlotte Goldstein, Sam Josephson, Frank Shechtman, Bertha Hart, Saul Josephson, Abraham Lax, Mike Wilensky, Morris B. Samuylow.

*The Sacrifice of Isaac.* H. Malkin, 1932.
   From *Sodome and Gomora* by Abraham Goldfadden.
   CAST: Adolph Gartner, Jennie Gartner, Eddie Friedlander, S. Gertensang, F. Adler, Sam Gertler, David Yanover, Max Friedlander.

*Shir Hashirim (Song of Songs).* Globe Pictures, 1935.
   Producer and director, Henry Lynn; story, Ansel Schorr; screenplay, Henry Lynn; music, Joseph Rumshinsky.
   CAST: Samuel Goldenberg, Dora Weissman, Max Kietter, Merele Gruber, Seymour Rechtzeit, Yudel Dubinsky.

*Shulamith.* Judea Films, 1931.
   Author and screenplay, Abraham Goldfadden.

*The Singing Blacksmith.* Collective Film Producers, 1938, 116 min.
   Director, Edgar G. Ulmer; based on *Yankel der Schmidt* by David Pinski; adaptation, David Pinski; screenplay, Ben-Tsvi Baratoff, Ossip Dymov; music, Jacob Weisberg; camera, William Miller.
   CAST: Moishe Oysher, Miriam Riselle, Florence Weiss, Anna Appel, Ben-Tsvi Baratoff, Michael Goldstein, Leah Noemi, Max Vodnoy, Lube Wesob, Yudel Dubinsky, Luba Rymers, Benjamin Fishbein, Rubin Wendroff, Herschel Bernardi, Ray Schneider, Sophie Bressler, Libby Charney, Clara Deutschmann, Janet Deutschmann, R. Shanock, Risa Halpern.

# FILMOGRAPHY

*The Sorrow of Israel.* Victor Film Company, Universal-Imp, 1913, 3 reels, silent.
Producer, Mark Dintenfass; director, Sidney Goldin.

*Tevya.* Mayman Films, Inc., 1939, 100 min.
Producer, Henry Ziskin; director, Maurice Schwartz; based on the stories by Sholom Aleichem; screenplay, Maurice Schwartz; music, Sholem Secunda; camera, Larry Williams; editor, Sam Citron; sets, William Saulter; sound, Paul Robillard.
CAST: Maurice Schwartz, Miriam Riselle, Paula Lubelska, Leon Liebgold, Vicky Marcus, Perle Marcus, Julius Adler, David Makarenko, Helen Gross, Morris Strassberg, Louis Weissberg, Al Hariss, Boaz Young.

*Three Daughters.* Cinema Service Corporation, 1961.
Director, Joseph Seiden.
CAST: Michael Rosenberg, Sacha Shaw, Rebecca Weintraub, Charlotte Goldstein, Max Wilner, Anatole Winogradoff, Jacob Schater.

*Two Sisters.* Graphic Picture Productions, 1938, 79 min.
Director, Ben K. Blake; story and screenplay, Samuel H. Cohen; music, Joseph Rumshinsky; camera, George F. Hinner; editor, Harry Foster.
CAST: Jennie Goldstein, Sylvia Dell, Muni Serebroff, Michael Rosenberg, Betty Bialis, John Carrol, Harvey Keir, Jack Wexler, Betty Jacobs, A. Teitlebaum, Rebecca Weintraub, Celia Budkin, Anna Levine, Ida Adler.

*Uncle Moses.* Yiddish Talking Pictures, Inc., 1932, 96 min.
Directors, Sidney Goldin and Aubrey Scotto; based on the novel by Sholem Asch.
CAST: Maurice Schwartz, Judith Abarbanol, R. Goldberg, Tzvi Schoder.

*Uriel Acosta.* Great Players Film Corporation, 1914, 5 reels, silent.
Director, Sidney Goldin.
CAST: Ben Adler, Rosetta Conn.

*A Vilna Legend.* Jewish Films Distributors, 1933.
Director, George Roland (sound); Zygmund Turkow (silent);

screenplay, Jacob Mestel (sound); Henryk Bojm (silent); camera, Seweryn Steinwurzel (silent).
  CAST (sound): Joseph Buloff, Jacob Mestel, Louis Kadison, Ben Bosenko, Benjamin Fishbein.
  CAST (silent): Esther Rachel Kaminska, Ida Kaminska, Moishe Lipman, Henryk Tarlo, Wladyslaw Godik, Zygmund Turkow, Samuel Landau, David Lederman, Lev Mogilov, Simcha Balanoff, Ruth Turkow.
Rereleased 1949.
Recut version of *Tkijes Khaf*. Leo-Forbert, 1924, Poland.

*The Voice of Israel*. Judea Films, 1930.
  Directors, Joseph Seiden, Asher Chasin.
  CAST: Seidel Rovner, Yossele Rosenblatt, Mordecai Herschman, David Rothman, Joseph Shilsky, Adolph Katchke, Cantor Leibele Waldman, Joseph Shapiro, Shaile Englehart, Cantor Meyer Machtenburg's Choir.

*The Wandering Jew*. Jewish American Film Art., Inc., 1933, 68 min.
  Director, George Roland; story, adaptor, dialogue, Jacob Mestel; music, I. J. Hochman; camera, Frank Zukor, J. Bergi Cotner.
  CAST: Jacob Ben-Ami, Morris B. Samuylow, Natalie Browning, Ben Adler, Jacob Mestel, Abraham Teitelbaum.
Rereleased 1938 as *A Jew in Exile*.

*What a Mother-in-Law*. Cinema Service Corporation, 1940, 66 min.
  CAST: Ludwig Satz, Jacob Mestel, Max Wilner.

*Where Is My Child? (Vu Is Mine Kind?)*. Menorah Productions, 1937, 80 min.
  Producer, Abraham Leff; directors, Henry Lynn and Abraham Leff; story, *Forgotten Mothers* by Sam Steinberg and William Segal; screenplay, Henry Lynn; camera, J. Burgi Cotner.
  CAST: Celia Adler, Anna Lillian, Morris Strassberg, Rubin Wendroff, Morris Silberkanter, Blanche Bernstein, Mischa Stuckchkoff, Cirel Arnod, S. Steinberg, Esther Gorber, Leo Schechtman.

*Yiddish King Lear*. 1935, 70 min.
  Producers, Johnny Walker and Jack Rieger; director, Harry

Thomashevsky; based on the play by Jacob Gordin; screenplay, Abraham Armband; camera, Joseph Freeman; recording engineer, Murray Dichter; supervised by Joseph Seiden.
CAST: Maurice Krohner, Fannie Levenstein, Jeannette Paskewitch, Esther Adler, Morris Weisman, Morris Tarlofsky, Jacob Bergreen, Eddie Pascal, Rose Rosen, Harold Shutzman, Roibelle.

*Yiddishe Fater (Jewish Father).* 60 min.
Producer, Jacob Silberman; director, Henry Lynn.
CAST: Wolf Goldfadden, Gertrude Bulman, Sam Gertier, Dave Fafer, Morris Strassberg, Itzak Swerdlev, Rose Wallerstein, Boaz Young, Dora Kashinskya, Moishe Zilberstein, Louis Bakshiksyky, Morris Marcus, Valie Valentimova, Alex Balshakov, Nadia Gorel, Esta Salzman, Harry Miller, Meyer Sikzer, Chai Yen.

*The Youth of Russia.* Sov-Am, 1934.
Director, Henry Lynn; screenplay, Henry Lynn; music, J. Stillman.
CAST: Wolf Goldfadden, Gertrude Bulman, Sam Gertler, Boaz Young, Dora Kashinskya, Rose Wallerstein, Morris Marcus, Yiddish Art Theater Players.

*Zein Weibs Lubovnik (His Wife's Lover).* High Art Pictures, 1931, 79 min.
Producers, Nathan Hirsch and Morris Kleinerman; director, Sidney Goldin; story and screenplay, S. R. Simkhof; music, Ludwig Satz; libretto, S. R. Simkhof; camera, Frank Zukor; editor, Joe Silverstein; recording engineer, Percy Glen.
CAST: Ludwig Satz, Lucy Levin, Isidor Cashier, Lillian Feinman, Zita Matkar, Michael Rosenberg, Jacob Frank.

## Documentaries

*The Dream of My People.* Palestine-American Film Co., Ltd., 1934.
Producer, Joseph Fox.
CAST: Cantor Yossele Rosenblatt.

*How the Jews Care for Their Poor.* Victor Film Company, Universal-Imp, 1913, 2 reels, silent.
Director, Sidney Goldin; story, Benjamin H. Namm and Max Abelman.

*The Jews in Poland.* The Jewish Pictures Corporation, 1920, silent. Travelogue.

*The Land of Promise (Chayim Chadasm).* Keren Kayemet, JNF, 1934, 45 min.
  Producer, Leo Herman; screenplay, Maurice Samuel; music, Boris Morris; songs, Natan A. Herman; narration, David Ross.

*Land of Promise.* Urim Palestine Film Company, 1936, 22 min.
  Director, Yehuda Lerman; camera, Charles W. Herbert; narration, Christopher Stone.

## Shorts

*Broken Doll.* Judea Films, 1930, 1 reel.
  Director, Joseph Seiden; author, Ivan Bussatt.
  CAST: Sadie Franks.

*Cantor Malevsky Series.* Cinema Service Corporation, 1949, 10 min.
  CAST: Cantor Malevsky and his Family Choir.

*A Cantor on Trial.* Judea Films, 1931, 1 reel.
  Producer, Jacob Berkowitz; director, Sidney Goldin; dialogue, Isadore Lillian.

*Chicken.*
  Music, Ruben Doctor.

*Eli, Eli.* Judea Films, 1930, 1 reel.
  Author, Sholem Secunda.
  CAST: Cantor Leibele Waldman.

*An Evening in a Jewish Camp.* Judea Films, 1930, 12 min.
  Authors, Sholem Secunda, Joseph Seiden.
  CAST: Eva Miller, Tama Miller.

*The Feast of Passover (Die Seder Nacht).* Standard Film Exchange, 1931, 2 reels.

Producer, Jacob Berkowitz; director, Sidney Goldin; dialogue, M. Schorr.
CAST: Cantor Leibele Waldman, Noah Nachbush, Mark Schweid, The Vilna Troupe.

*Hayom Horas Oylom,* Jewish Talking Pictures Company, Inc., 1937, 10 min.
CAST: Cantor Mordechai Hershman.

*I Want to Be a Boarder.* Jewish Talking Pictures Company, Inc., 1937, 35 min.
Producer and director, Joseph Seiden.
CAST: Leo Fuchs, Yetta Zwerling.

*Jewish Day Hour.* Judea Films, 1930, 2 reels.
Authors, Z. Rubenstein, Joseph Seiden.

*Jewish Gypsy.* Judea Films, 1930, 21 min.
Author, Hymie Jacobson.
CAST: Hymie Jacobson.

*Jewish Melody.* Judea Films, 1930, 1 reel.
Author, Sholem Secunda.
CAST: Cantor Leibele Waldman.

*Kol Nidre I & II.* Judea Films, 1930, 2 reels.
Authors, Samuel Gottsman, Cantor Leibele Waldman.
CAST: Cantor Leibele Waldman.

*Land of Freedom.* Judea Films, 1930, 2 reels.
Author, Seymour Rechtzeit.

*Mai-ko-mashmalon.* Judea Films, 1930, 1 reel.
Author, Abraham Raizin.
CAST: Harry Feld.

*Moishe Oysher Sings.* Cinema Service Corporation.
CAST: Moishe Oysher.

*My Grandfather's Dream.* Cinema Service Corporation.
CAST: Cantor Leibele Waldman.

*Natascha.* Judea Films, 1930, 2 reels.
Author, Pincus Lavenda.

*Oy! Doctor.* Judea Films, 1930, 2 reels.
Author, Isadore Lillian.
CAST: Menasha Skulnick.

*Sailor's Sweetheart.* Judea Films, 1930, 2 reels.
Screenplay, Hymie Jacobson.

*Shoemaker's Romance.* Judea Films, 1930, 2 reels.
Director, Sidney Goldin; author, Louis Kadison; art director, Van Rosen.
CAST: Leah Noemi, Leon Kadison, Liuba Kadison, Joseph Buloff.

*Shulamith.* Judea Films, Inc., 1931, 1 reel.
Author, Abraham Goldfadden.

*Stars Are Singing.* Cinema Service Corporation.
CAST: Aaron Lebedoff, Anna Lubin, Max Wilner, Pincus Lavenda, Hymie Jacobson, Miriam Krasner.

*Style and Class.* Judea Films, 1930, 23 min.
Director, Sidney Goldin; author, Marty Baratz; art director, Van Rosen.
CAST: Marty Baratz, Goldie Eisman, Boris Rosenthal, Ida Goldstein.

*Unsana Takeff.* Judea Films, 1930, 1 reel.
Author, Sholem Secunda.
CAST: Cantor Leibele Waldman, Meyer Machtenburg, Cantor Yossele Rosenblatt.

### Miscellaneous

*The Earth Cries Out.* Italy, 1949, 80 min.
Producer, Albert Salvator; director, Dulic Coletti; screenplay, Lewis F. Gittler.
CAST: Andrea Cheechi, Ludgidtos, Peter Trent, Maria Beri, Vivi Gio.

*We Live Again.* Jewish Film Distributors, France, 1948, 53 min.
 Producers, M. Banhelfer and O. Fessler, A. Hamza, I. Iolodenko, H. Weinfeld.

# Index

Page numbers in italics refer to illustrations.

Aaron Film Corporation, 118. *See also* Cinema Service Corporation; Jewish Talking Pictures Company, Inc.; Judea Film Corporation
Abarbonal, Judith, 89, 93
*Abie's Irish Rose* (play), 101
Abramovich, Shalom Jacob [pseud. Seforim, Mendele Mocher], 28, 51, 88
Abramson, Ivan, 58
Academy of Motion Pictures Arts and Sciences, 110
Adelheim, Tamara, 46
Adler, Ben, 40, 97
Adler, Celia, 17, 95, *96*
Adler, Julius, 55
Adler, S., 33
Agudath Israel, 52–53
*Al Chet (I Have Sinned)*, 110, 112, 137
Aleichem, Sholom. *See* Rabinowitz, Solomon
"America" (song), 80
American Jewish Historical Society, 120
American Mutoscope and Biograph Company, 34
American Relief Expedition, 58
*Americaner Schadchen (The American Matchmaker)*, 26, 89, 91–93, *92*, 118, 144
Amkino, 70
Anski, S. *See* Rapoport, Shloyme Zalmen
*Anthony in the Capital*, 31
*Avram Ovenu. See Eternal Jew, The*
Appel, Anna, 55, 64, 91
Arkatov, Alexander, 30, 45
Armat, Thomas, 34
Artef, 84
Asch, Sholem, 30, 70
Audio Branden Films, 118

Babel, Isaac, 48–50, 56
Baheifer, M., 117
Balaban, Meyer, 112
*Bar Mitzvah*, 94, 96, 104, 118, 144
Baratz, Marty, 59, 62
Batalov, Nikolai, 71
Beilis, Mendel, 28

*Beilis Case The (Delo Beilisa)*, 45, 133
Ben-Ami, Jacob, 70, 83–84, 118
*Benya Krik*, 48, 133
Berger, Gustav, 118
Berliner, Sam, 59, 62
Bernardi, Herschel, 84, *85*, 87–88
Berne, Joseph, 25, 99, 118
*Beser dem Tot oder aza Shand (Better Death Than Shame)*, 30, 133
Best Films, 114
Beverly, Helen, 17, 88, 91
*Bezhin Meadow*, 50
Bialik, Chaim Nachman, 28
*Bigamistka*. See *Zajn Wajbs Man* (1913)
*Birobidjan*. See *Seekers of Happiness*
*Black Cat, The*, 83
Black Hundred. See League of Russian People
*Black 107, The*, 39–40, 145
Blake, Ben K., 100
*Bleeding Hearts or Jewish Freedom under King Casimir of Poland*, 37–38, 145
Block, Mildred, 61
*Bloody Jest, The (Der Blutiken Shpas)*, 45, 133
Bloom, Lillian, 97
Blumenfeld, Dina, 52
*Bog, Człowiek I Szatan*. See *God, Man and Devil* (Poland)
Bojm, Henryk, 52
Bonn, Ferdinand, 53
Box Office Attraction Company, 41
Boyle, Irene, 40
Bozhyk, Max, 118
*Brivele der Manen, A (A Little Letter to Mother)* (Poland), 108–10, 118, 137
*Brivele der Manen, A* (Soviet Union), 30, 133
Brodsky, Nicholas, 25, 108

*Broken Doll*, 62, 156
*Broken Hearts*, 55–56, 68, 145
*Brooklyn Daily Eagle*, 74–75
Brooklyn Federation of Jewish Charities, 38–39
Bulman, Gertrude, 94
Buloff, Joseph, 59, 107
Bund, the, 28, 44, 87
Bureau of Education of the Jewish Community of New York, 40
Burstyn, Joseph, 72

Cahan, Abe, 85, 110
*Cain and Artem*, 50, 134
Camp Siegfried. See Bund, the
*Cantor Malevsky Series*, 156
*Cantor on Trial, A*, 156
*Cantor's Son, The*, 100, 103, 145
Carmel Productions, 88
Carter, Lincoln J., 35
Cashier, Isidore, 17, 25, 55, 79, 88, 91
*Castles in the Air*. See *Yiddle with His Fiddle*
*Catskill Honeymoon*, 118, 145
*Chalutzim*, 69, 112, 118
Champion Studios, 36
Chasin, Asher, 66
*Chazon, Der*. See *Overture to Glory*
*Chazons Tochter, Dem (The Cantor's Daughter)*, 32, 137
Chenkin, Victor, 99
*Chicken*, 156
*Children Must Laugh*. See *Mir Kumen On*
*Children of the Ghetto, The*, 41, 146
*Chinese Mill, The*, 48
Cinema Service Corporation, 74, 114, 118–20. See also Aaron Film Corporation; Jewish Talking Pictures Company, Inc.; Judea Film Corporation
*City in Poland*, 143

# INDEX

*Cleveland Jewish Independent*, 41
Cohen, Samuel H., 100
Collective Film Producers, 84, 87
*Comrade Abram*, 46
Conn, Rosetta, 40
*Córka Kantora*. See *Chazons Tochter, Dem*
Cotner, J. Burgi, 25, 70
Credo Films, 99
Criterion Laboratory, 77
Cultkino, 48
Cutler, Yosel, 72

*Daughter of Her People, A*, 68, 137, 146
de Bree, Sybille, 53
Defender Films, 29
Dell, Sylvia, 100
*Deluge, The* (book), 47
*Destruction of Jerusalem, The*, 66
*Detroit Jewish Chronicle, The*, 64
Dintenfass, Mark M., 36–37
*Don Juan*, 55
Drankov, Alexander O., 29
*Dream of My People, The*, 68, 155
Dubinsky, David, 85
Dubinsky, Yudel, 61, 88
*Dudele, A (A Home Spun Melody)*, 146
*Dybbuk, The*, 25, 94, 103, 112–14, *113*, 118, 138
*Dybbuk, The* (play), 66, 94
Dymov, Ossip, 25, 99
Dzigan, Shimon, 25, 110, *111*, 112, 114, 117

*Earth Cries Out, The*, 117, 158
*East Side Sadie*, *63*, 64, 72, 146
Eclair Studios, 53
Edison Company, 34
Einbinder, Gershon (pseud. Paver, Chaver), 88
Eisenstein, Sergei, 50
Eisman, Goldie, 59
Ekran Film, 53

*Eli, Eli*, 79, 146
*Eli, Eli* (short), 146
Elite Productions, Inc., 99
Ellis, Jack, 64
Ellstein, Abe, 106, 109
Elvy, Maurice, 97
Epstein, Sadell, 61
Eron Pictures, 100
*Escaped from Siberia*, 40, 146
Essany Film Manufacturing Company, 34–35
*Eternal Fools*, 61–62, 146–47
*Eternal Jew, The*, 68, 69, 147
*Eternal Prayer, The (Ad Mosae)*, 64, 72, 147
*Evening in a Jewish Camp, An*, 156

*Feast of Passover, The (Die Seder Nacht)*, 156–57
Feld, Esther, 95
Feld, Harry, 80
Fencke Films, 112
*Fersztoyśene, Di (The Disinherited)*, 32, 138
Fessler, O., 117
*Fiddler on the Roof*, 24
*Film Daily* (New York), 64, 101, 102
*Film Daily Yearbook*, 17
*Film Index, The*, 29
Film Polski, 21, 116, 117
Finkelstein, Henryk, 32
*Fishke der Krumer (Fishke the Lame)* (book), 88
Fishzon, Mischa, 33
Forbert, Leo. See Leo-Forbert Films
Ford, Alexander, *69*, 112
*Forgotten Mothers* (play), 95, 154
*Forward, The* (New York), 34, 54, 83, 85, 108, 110
Fox, William, 41
Freed, Lazar, 79
*Freiheit* (New York), 83
Fuchs, Leo, 25, 77–79, 89, 91–93, *92*

*Führe Uns Nicht in Versuchung (Lead Us Not into Temptation),* 53

Gartner, Adolph, 64, 66–67
Gartner, Jennie, 67
Gaumont, 28–29
Gehrman, Lucy, 108–10
Gehrman, Mischa, 108–10
General Film Company. *See* Motion Picture Patents Company
Gersten, Berta, 99
Ginsberg, Samuel, 32
Globe Pictures, 117
*God, Man and Devil* (Poland), 32, 138
*God, Man and Devil* (United States), 118, 147
*God of Vengeance,* 30, 134
Goldberg, Joseph, 116
Goldenberg, Samuel, 61, 94–95
Goldfadden, Abraham, 105
Goldfadden, Wolf, 55, 94
Goldfadden Troupe, 108
Goldin, Bertina, 64
Goldin, Sidney M., 35–40, 53–54, 56, 58, 60, 62, 64, 66, 72, 100
Goldin Films, 53
Goldman, Moe, 59, 61–62
Goldman, Pawel, 32
Goldstein, Jennie, 61, 100
Goldstein, Michael, 84, *85*
Goldstein, Samuel, 67
Goldstein, Zena, 97
Goldsztein, Zina, 32
*Golem, The* (play), 47, 67
Gordin, Jacob, 32–33, 99–100, 110, *111*, 112, 118
GOSET (Jewish People's Theater), 46, 50, 52, 72
Goskind, Shaul, 69, 110–12, 116–17
Goskind, Yitzak, 69, 110–12
Goskino, 48
*Gots Sztrof (God's Punishment),* 32, 138

Granowski, Alexis, 25, 46–47
*Great Advisor, The (Der Groyseretz Gever),* 79, 82–83, 118, 147
Great Players Feature Film Company, 40
*Greater Promise, A. See Seekers of Happiness*
Green, Joseph, 66–68, 73–74, 86, 89, 97, 102, 104–10, 114–15, 117–18
*Green Fields (Greene Felder),* 26, 83–89, *85*, 93, 99
*Green Fields (Greene Felder)* (play), 83
Greene, Ira, 99–100
Greenfield, Rose, 75, 79
Gritcher, Gregory, 46, 48, 50
Gross, Helen, 114
Gross, Natan, 117
*Guardsman, The* (play), 66
Gudinsky, Bella, 61
Guskin, Reuben, 60
Gutman, David, 71
Gutzkow, Karl F., 40

Habimah, 45–47, 50
Halpern, Dina, 114
Hamza, A., 117
Hansen, Kai, 30
*Happy Times. See Live and Laugh*
*Hasa die Yesome (Hasa the Orphan)* (Lipovski), 33, 138
*Hasa die Yesome (Hasa the Orphan)* (Vilna Circle Theater), 33, 138
*Hayom Horas Oylom,* 157
*Heart of a Jewess, The,* 37, 148
Hebrew Actors Union, 60, 76
Hebrew Immigrant Aid Society (HIAS), 108–9
Helio-Film, 53
*Her Second Mother,* 77, 80–81, 114, 148
*Herecle Mejuches,* 33, 138
Hertz, Alexander, 31

# INDEX

High Art Picture Corporation, 66
Hirschbein, Peretz, 83–84
Hirsh, Nathan, 66
Holdenka, I., 117
Hollander, Hannah, 79
Hollywood Yiddish Film Corporation, 100
Holtzer, Rachel, 110
*Holy Oath, The*, 148
*Horizon, the Wandering Jew*, 71
*How the Jews Care for Their Poor*, 38–39, 155
*How the Steel Was Tempered*, 50
*Hütet Eure Töchter (Protect Your Daughters)*, 53

*I Want to Be a Boarder*, 78, 157
*I Want to Be a Mother*, 77–79, 81, 102, 148
*Idle Inn*, 88
*If I Were Rothschild (Ven Ich Bin Roytshild)*, 45, 134
*Ihre Vergangenheit (Her Past)*, 53
Imp, The (Independent Motion Picture Company), 35–36
International Ladies Garment Workers Union (ILGWU), 85–86
Ivanov-Barkov, Yevgeni, 47

Jacobs, Lewis, 99
Jacobson, Hymie, 62
Jaffe, Louis N., 55–56
Jaffe Art Films, 55–56
*Jazz*. See *Puppets*
*Jazz Singer, The*, 55
*Jeden Z 36*. See *Lamedvovnik, Der*
*Jew at War, A*, 50–51, 134
*Jew in Exile, A*. See *The Wandering Jew* (United States)
*Jew on the Land, The*, 71–72, 134
Jewish American Film Art, Inc., 70
Jewish Art Players (Poland), 117
*Jewish Day Hour*, 157
Jewish Film Distributors, 118

*Jewish Gypsy*, 62, 157
*Jewish Luck*. See *Matchmaker, The*
*Jewish Melody, The*, 79, 80, 114, 118, 148
*Jewish Melody* (short), 62, 79, 157
Jewish National Fund, 70
Jewish Picture Corporation, 55
Jewish Talking Pictures Company, Inc., 74. See also Aaron Film Corporation, Cinema Service Corporation, Judea Film Corporation
Jewish Telegraphic Agency, 62, 64
*Jewish Queen Lear*. See *Mirele Efros* (United States)
*Jewish Regiment (Evereisky Polk)*, 46, 134
*Jewish Song, The*. See *Jewish Melody, The*
Jewison, Norman, 24
*Jews in Poland, The* (United States), 55, 156
*Jews in Poland* (Poland), 117, 143
*Jimmy Higgins* (book), 48
Joint Distribution Committee, 66, 116
*Jolly Paupers (Freyliche Kabtsonim)*, 111, 112, 139
*Joseph and His Brethren*, 64, 66, 149
*Joseph in the Land of Egypt*, 67–68, 101–2, 104, 149
Judea Film Corporation, 57, 59, 61–62, 74–77. See also Aaron Film Corporation, Cinema Service Corporation, Jewish Talking Pictures Company, Inc.
*Juden von Toledo, Die (The Jews of Toledo)*, 53
*Judenmädel, Das (The Jewish Girl)*, 53, 143
*Judge, People*, 45, 134
Judische-Kuntsfilm, 54

Kacynzna, A. S., 112
*Kaddish*, 66

Kalem Company, The, 34–35, 40–41
Kalich, Jacob, 53–54, 105, 109
Kaminska, Esther Rachel, 31–33
Kaminska, H., 33
Kaminska, Ida, 32, 52, *111*, 117
Kaminsky, Avrom Yitskhok, 31
Kaminsky Troupe, 25, 31–33
*Kansas City Jewish Chronicle*, 103
*Kara Boža*. See *Gots Sztrof*
Kerman Films, 54
Khanzhonkov, 30
*Kiddish Hashem*, 31, 134
*King Lear*, 30
*King of Kings*, 66
*Kltashe, Di*. See *Light Ahead, The*
Kleine, George, 34
Kleinerman, Morris, 66
*Kol Nidre*, 149
*Kol Nidre I & II* (short), 62, 157
"Kol Nidre" (song), 99
Korsh-Sablin, Vladimir, 71
*Kosher Dance*. See *Puppets*
Kosmofilm, 32–33
Kreisler, Otto, 53
Krohner, Maurice, 101
Kuleshov, Lev, 71

Lackay, Wilton, 41
*Lai Chyeim (Good Luck)*, 30, 134
*Lamedvovnik, Der (One of the 36)*, 52, 139
*Land of Freedom*, 157
*Land of Promise*, 70, 156
*Land of Promise, The (Chayim Chadism)*, 68, 70, 156
Landy, Ludwig, 99–100
*Laughter through Tears*, *49*, 50, 72, 135
Lawrence, Florence, 35
Lax, Abraham, 25
League of Russian People, 29, 39–40, 47–48
*Lebediker Yusem, Der*. See *My Son*

Lee, Lila, 55
Leo Films, 52
Leo-Forbert Films, 52, 56
Leone, Henri, 40
Leonidoff, Leonid M., 50
Levin, Lucy, 64
*Leybe der Shuster (Leybe the Shoemaker)*, 139
Libin, Zalmen, 32
*Light Ahead, The*, 25, 88–89, 91, 93–94, 101–2
Liliana, Lili, *113*
Lillian, Isidore, 62
Lipovsky, Nahum, 33
Listo Films, 54
Littman's People's Theater, 103
*Live and Laugh*, 149
*Living Corpse, The*, 61
*Living Orphan, The*. See *My Son*
Loew's Theaters, 86, 107
Lopert, Illya, 85
*Love and Passion* (book), 75
*Love and Sacrifice (Liebe un Leidenschaft)*, 75, 79, 118, 150
Lynn, Henry, 94–97, *96*, 102, 104, 114

*Mabul*, 47–48, 135
Machtenberg, Meyer, 61
*Macocha*. See *Sztifmuter, Di*
*Mai-ko-mashmalon*, 157
Makarenko, David, *98*
*Małzenstwona Rozdrozu*. See *Zajn Wajbs Man* (1916)
*Mamele (Little Mother)*, 109–10, 118, 139
Manger, Itzik, 106
Marten, Alexander, 32
Masimon, Shalom, 40
*Masters and Workers*, 33, 139
*Matchmaker, The*, 46, 72, 135
Maurice Schwartz's Jewish Art Theater, 25, 55, 66, 83
*Mayerling*, 86

*Mazel Tov (Good Luck)*, 53–54, 144
*Mazel Tov, Yidden (Congratulations, Jews)*, 78, *119*, 150
Mecca Film Laboratories, Inc., 100
Melies's Star Films, 34
*Menachem Mendel* (book), 46
Mercury Film, 77
Mestel, Jacob, 68, 70, 112
Mesterland, Jacob, 118
Metropolitan Studios, 64
Meyer, Fidelson, 86
Meyer, Georges. *See* Mundviller, Joseph
Michalesko, Michael, 118
Mikhoels, Shlomo, 25, 30, 46, 71–72
Mintus Company, The, 33
*Mir Kumen On (We Arrive)*, 69, 112, 143
*Mirele Efros* (Poland), 32, 139
*Mirele Efros* (Soviet Union), 135
*Mirele Efros* (United States), 99, 101, 150
*Mirelebn Gerlebn (We Live Again)*, 117, 143
*Moishe Oysher Sings*, 157
Molnár, Ferenc, 66
*Monticello Here We Come*, 118, 150
Moscow Jewish Art Theater. *See* GOSET
*Moscow Nights*, 47
*Motel Peyse, the Cantor's Son. See Laughter through Tears*
*Motel the Operator*, 79, 81–82, *82*, 118, 150–51
*Motel the Weaver (Motele Shpinder)*, 48, 135
*Mothers of Today*, 95, 102, 151
*Motion Picture Daily, The*, 110
Motion Picture Patents Company, 20, 34–35
Motyleff, Illya, 100
Movielab, 77
*Moving Picture World*, 33, 37

Mozhukhin, Ivan, 30
Mundviller, Joseph [pseud. Meyer, Georges), 30–31
Muni, Paul, 25
*My Grandfather's Dream*, 157
*My Son*, 80, 151
*My Yiddishe Mama*, 25, 60–62, 64, 151

*Natascha*, 158
*Neighbors*, 114, 118, 140
*New York Dramatic Mirror*, 30, 38, 41
*New York Herald Tribune*, 86
*New York Telegraph*, 57
*New York Times*, 39, 86, 98, 101, 110
*Newsweek*, 114
*Nieznajomy. See Unbekanter, Der*
*Nihilist Vengeance*, 36, 151
Nihilists, 36, 40
Noemi, Leah, 59
Nosseck, Martin, 99
Nosseck, Max, 25, 99
Nugent, Frank, 86

*Odessa Tales, The* (book), 48
*Okrutny Ojciec. See Vilder Fater, Der*
Opatoshu, David, 23, 25, 88, 91
Opatoshu, Joseph, 52
*Oppenheim Family, The*, 71
Osherwitz, M., 108
*Ost und West. See Mazel Tov*
Ostrowsky, Nikolai Alexayevich, 50
*Overture to Glory*, 96, 99, 100, 117, 151
*Oy! Doctor*, 158
Oysher, Moishe, 25, 87–88, *90*, 99, 100, 101, 117

Palestine-American Film Company, 67

*Paradise in Harlem*, 58
*Passover Miracle, A*, 40–41, 151
Pathé Frères, 28–31, 34–35, 45
Paver, Chaver. *See* Einbinder, Gershon
*Peasant Women of Ryazan*, 50
*People Eternal A*, 97, 152
*Peppery Jews*. *See Puppets*
Peretz, I. L., 28, 45, 51
Pica, Jean, 86
Picon, Molly, 25, 53–54, 83–84, 105–7, 109, 117–18
Pictorial Ventures, 118
*Piętro Wyžej. See Neighbors*
*Pilots*, 48
Pinski, David, 87
*Pintele Yid, Dos*, 33, 140
Polish State Film Studios. *See* Film Polski
*Polish Woods, [In the] (W Lasach Polskich)*, 52–53, 140
*Portland Scribe, The*, 62
Powell, Frank, 41
*Power of Life, The*, 95, 152
Preobrazhenskaya, Olga, 50
Proletkino, 48
*Prototypes of the Protocols of the Elders of Zion* (book), 28
Pryes, Ludwig, 112
Przybilski, Jan-Nowina, 25, 106
*Prsysiega* (book), 33
*Puppets*, 72, 137
*Purimspieler, Der (The Jester)*, 102, 107–8, 118, 140

Rabinowitz, Solomon [pseud. Aleichem, Shalom], 28, 45–48, 50–51, 56, 81–82, *82*, 97, 101
Raizin, Abraham, 62
Rapoport, Sholyme Zalmen [pseud. Anski, S.], 51, 81, 112–14
Rebush, Roman, 84, 99
Reichtzeit, Seymour, 62, 79
*Return of Nathan Becker, The*, 71, 136

*Review of the Troops by the Royal Family at Tsarkoye Selo*, 29
Rich, Silven, 52
Richter, Moshe, 33
Rieger, Jack, 100
Riselle, Miriam, 97
*Riverside Drive*, 88
Rivling and Company (Tel Aviv), 61
Rokeach, Vice-Mayor (Tel Aviv), 61
Roland, George, 68, 70, 77, 112, 118
Room, Abram, 71
Rosen, Sam, 99
Rosenberg, Michael, 50, 72, 100, 118
Rosenblatt, Max, 97
Rosenblatt, Yossele, 61, 68
Rosenthal, Boris, *63*, 64
Roshal, Grigori, 50–51, 71
Rubenstein, Mr. (editor of *Der Tog*), 89
Rubinstein, Lewis J., 39
Ruby Feature Film Company, 39
*Russian Father*, 136
*Russia, the Land of Oppression*, 29
Rutenberg and Everett Yiddish Film Library, 120

*Sacrifice of Isaac, The* (Soviet Union), 30
*Sacrifice of Isaac, The* (United States), 68, 102, 152
*Sailor's Sweetheart*, 158
Salter, Harry, 35
Salzman, Esta, 80
Satz, Ludwig, 79
Scenic Studio, 59
Schecter, Leon, 97
Schildkraut, Joseph, 66
Schildkraut, Rudolph, 66, 83
Schmulikel, 64
Schumacher, Israel, 25, 110, *111*, 112, 114, 117

# INDEX

Schwartz, Maurice, 17, 25, 54–56, 66, 68, 70, 73, *76*, 84, 89, 97–98, *98*, 105
Schwartz, Max, 80
Schweid, Mark, *63*
Sebel, Stanislaw, 32–33
Secunda, Sholem, 62, 79
*Seeds of Freedom*, 50, 136
*Seekers of Happiness*, 71–72, 136
Seforim, Mendele Mocher. *See* Abramovich, Shalom Jacob
Segal, William, 95
Seiden, Harold, 77–78, 119–20
Seiden Joseph [pseud. Zeiden, Joseph], 21, 23, 58–64, 66, 68, *69*, 72–75, 77–83, *82*, 89–90, *90*, 94, 99, 101–2, 114, 116, 118–20, *119*
Seiden Studios of the Talking Picture, 74
Sektor, 110–12
Selig Polyscope Company, The, 34
Serebroff, Muni, 80, 100
Shearer, Douglas, 24
*Shir Hashirim (Song of Songs)*, 94–95, 152
*Shma Yisroel*, 33, 141
*Shoemaker's Romance*, 59, 158
*Shop on Main Street*, 32
*Shulamith*, 62, 152
*Shulamith* (short), 158
Sieracki, Herman, 32
Sigmund Lubin Company, The, 34
Sikawitt, Mortimer D., 67
Sila Films, 32–33
Simkhoff, S. R., 66
Simon, Mae, 60
*Simonas and His Wife. See Puppets*
Sinclair, Upton, 48
Sinkoff, Abe, *63*
*Singing Blacksmith, The*, 87–91, *90*, 93, 103, 118
*Sing Molly Sing*, 143
*Skotinins, The*, 50
Skulnick, Menasha, 62

*Slaughter, The. See Szchite, Di*
Slavinsky, A., 33
Smoelski, Jan, 39
Soifer, Josef, 45
*Solemn Procession of Pilgrims at Kiev*, 29
*Sorrow of Israel, The*, 36, 153
*Sorrows of Sarah*, 30, 136
Sov-Am, 94
Soviet Film Studios, 70
Sovkino, 47
Sphinx Films, 104–5
*Stars Are Singing*, 158
Steinberg, Sam, 95
Steinwurcel, Seweryn, 52
*Story of the Bible, A. See Eternal Jew, The*
Stroyeva, Vera, 50
*Style and Class*, 59, 158
Szaro, Henry, 52, 112, 114
*Szchite, Di (The Slaughter)*, 32–33, 141
*Sztifmuter, Di (The Stepmother)*, 32, 141

Talmadge Studio, 124
Tauber, Chaim, *82*
*Tevya*, 25, *76*, 97–98, *98*, 101, 103, 105, 153
*Tevya and His Seven Daughters* (book), 97
*Theodor Herzl der Bannerträger (Theodore Herzl the Banner Carrier)*, 53
*Third State Duma in Session, The*, 29
Thomashevsky, Boris, 17–18, 25, 94, 104
Thomashevsky, Harry, 101
*Thou Shalt Remember. See Yiskor*
*Three Daughters*, 118, 153
*Time*, 114
*Tkijes Khaf (The Vow). See Vilna Legend*
*Tog, Der* (New York), 83, 89

Tostoy, Leo, 33, 61
Towbin, Mojzesz Morak, 32
Trans-Oceanic Film Company, 40
"Trust, The." See Motion Picture Patents Company
Turkow, Jonas, 52
Turkow, Zygmund, 52, 107–8, 114
*Two Sisters*, 100, 102, 153

*Ubój.* See *Szchite, Di*
Ulmer, Edgar G., 24, 83–94, *85*, *90*, *92*, 99, 101, 115
*Unbekantor, Der (The Stranger)*, 32, 141
*Uncle Moses*, 25, 70, 97, 102–3, 153
*Uncle Tom's Cabin*, 58
Undershalk, J., 50
*Unfortunate Bride of Suffolk Street, The.* See *Broken Hearts*
United Artists Theaters, 107
Universal Film Manufacturing Company, 35–39, 41, 58
*Universal Weekly*, 36
*Unsana Takeff*, 158
Unzer Theater, 66
*Unzere Kinder (Our Children)*, 116–17, 143
*Uriel Acosta*, 88
*Uriel Acosta* (silent), 40, 153
Urim Palestine Film Company, 70

*Variety* (New York), 39–40, 58, 87, 101
Variety Feature Film Company, 33
Vershilov, Boris Illyitch, 47
Victor Feature Film Company, 35–36, 55
*Vilder Fater, Der (The Cruel Father)*, 32, 141
Vilna Circle Theater, 33
*Vilna Legend, A*, 52, 68, 118, 153–54
Vilna Troupe, 18, 52, 66, 68
Vilner, Vladimir, 48
Vitagraph Company of America, The, 34

Vladimir Mendem Sanitarium, 112
*Voice of Israel, The*, 61, 64, 66, 70, 78, 154
*Vow, The*, 114, 118, 141
*Vu Iz Mein Hasa? (Where Is My Khasa?)*, 136
Vufku, 50

Waksman, E., 32
Waldman, Cantor Leibele, 61–62, 79, 82
Walker, Johnny, 100
Wallace, Irene, 37–38
*Wandering Jew, The* (United Kingdom), 97, 152
*Wandering Jew, The* (United States), 70, 154
*Wandering Stars*, 48, 136
*War and the Jew, The*, 30, 136
Warsaw Art Players, 110, 112, 114
Warsaw Yiddish Art Theater, 18, 23, 52
Wasilevska, Wanda, 112
Wasynski, Michael, 25, 112–13
Weinfeld, H., 117
Weisberg, Louis, 61
Weiss, Florence, *90*
*We Live Again*, 117, 159
*What a Mother-in-Law*, 79, 154
*Where Is My Child? (Vu Is Mine Kind?)*, 95, *96*, 154
*Without a Home (Ahn a Heim)*, *111*, 112, 142
World Art Film Company, 64
*Wydziedziczene.* See *Ferśztoysene, Di*

*Yankee Boile*, 88
*Yankel der Schmidt* (play), 87
*Yeshiva Bocher, Der*, 33, 142
Yeshiva College of America, 58
Yiddish Art Theater, 50
*Yiddish King Lear*, 100–101, 154–55
Yiddishe Bande, 102
*Yiddishe Fater (Jewish Father)*, 155

Yiddish Scientific Institute (YIVO), 116
*Yiddle with His Fiddle*, 24, 86, 103, 105–8, 110, 116, 118, 142
*Yiskor*, 54, 144
*Yom Hachupa (The Wedding Day)*, 33, 142
*Youth of Russia, The*, 94, 155

*Zajn Wajbs Man (His Wife's Man)* (1913), 32, 142
*Zajn Wajbs Man (His Wife's Man)* (1916), 33, 142
Zanger, Jacob, 79

Zangwill, Israel, 41
Zaswaski, Rudolf, 32
*Zein Weib's Lubovnik (His Wife's Lover)*, 65, 66, 155
Zeiden, Joseph. *See* Seiden, Joseph
Ziskin, Henry, 98
Zolatarefsky, Isadore, 75
Zukor, Frank, 70
Zuskin, Venyamin, 50
Zwerling, Yetta, 17, 79
*Zvay Musicanten (Two Musicians)*, 142
*Zvay Musicanten (Two Musicians)* (short), 143